THE UNOFFICIAL
HARRY
POTTER
VEGAN
COOKBOOK

IMANA GRASHUIS and TYLOR STARR
Foreword by Evanna Lynch

Table of Contents

Iconic Locales Guide

The recipes in this book are inspired by the many magical places Harry visits over the course of the *Harry Potter* series.

A CUPBOARD UNDER THE STAIRS
Harry's "bedroom" at Number 4 Privet Drive, the home of Aunt Petunia, Uncle Vernon and Dudley.

SCHOOLGROUND FEASTS
The enchanted room at Hogwarts in which students gather for daily meals, feasts and other events.

HERBOLOGY GREENHOUSE
Professor Sprout holds lessons here to help students gain hands-on experience with various plants.

DIVING INTO THE LAKE
An iconic feature of the Hogwarts grounds that Harry explores during the Triwizard Tournament.

WALTZING AT THE BALL
Hogwarts hosts this international soirée as part of the Triwizard Tournament festivities.

A FRIENDLY VISIT TO THE HALF-GIANT'S HUT
Hagrid's humble home, a warm, welcoming place for Harry and his friends.

INTO THE DARK CAVE: SOUL-SPLITTING CREATIONS
The sea cave in which Voldemort hides the locket Horcrux.

COMFORT COOKING FROM THE BURROW
The Weasley family home is where matriarch Molly cooks to feed a crowd.

STROLLING THROUGH A SNOW-CAPPED VILLAGE
Britain's only wizarding village, home to many beloved haunts.

COMMON (OR REQUIRED) ROOMS
Public spaces where students study, hang out or unwind between classes.

BREWING BUBBLING POTIONS IN THE DUNGEONS
Home to the Slytherin common room and Potions classrooms.

SPELLBINDING DELICACIES THROUGH THE BRICK WALL
AKA Diagon Alley, where Harry shops for school supplies.

MAGICAL TRANSPORTATION
The Knight Bus and Hogwarts Express, which help Harry and other wizards get around.

DEATH EATER DELIGHTS
Followers of the Dark Lord do not limit themselves to practicing the Dark Arts in any one place.

Look for these stamps throughout the book to uncover the connections between the recipes and the locations that inspired them!

Full Moon Cookies,
pg. 174

Foreword

**HEN I WAS YOUNGER, I** believed in all types of magic. I believed cats could talk but chose not to. I believed the eyes of my dolls shining through the night were watching me, closely studying the nuances of my behavior and playing at being human children while I slept, just as I played with their houses by daylight. I believed certain trees were completely hollow and fairies the size of paper clips with gossamer wings lived within their trunks. Chunks of bark would fall away, revealing small, ridged pieces of wood my eldest sister knowingly informed me were the tiny front doors of their cozy fairy enclaves. I'd crouch down in the grass and rap a tentative knuckle against these "doors," imagining the thundering knocks echoing through an entire community of fairies, their disgruntled little faces peeking out from between the curtains of tulip petals to grumble to one another about the oafish human child making such a racket outside, but hoping that one of them might find their curiosity piqued enough to poke a felt-hatted head out the front door. Sometimes the magic I believed in was scary; my second sister insisted a hungry sea witch lived beneath the toilet, that the roar of the flushing toilet was actually the sound of her cavernous, gurgling belly, and that if you loitered in the bathroom too long, her scaly hand would snake up through the pipes, snatch you around the waist and suck you down into her lair to feast on your flesh. It was everywhere, the magic: Silvery streams concealing secret entrances to fairytale kingdoms, if one could only find the key. Poisonous berries that would turn you into a bright orange toad

glinted ominously through the bushes, and I never found a friend reckless enough to try one. Oddly-shaped rocks grimaced unpleasantly because they were actually cursed princes, trapped in stone for their sins. Flowers sang. Trees muttered in the breeze. And one day, when I grew up, I'd sprout wings and notice iridescent dust trailing from my fingertips and I'd become a fairy, too—I just knew it.

I am not sure why, as we grow up, we cut ourselves off from the magic we embraced so naturally as children. Why, at a certain point, do we stop taking magic seriously? Perhaps it's too much possibility, too much to think about. Perhaps the notion that we can affect change in the world around us with our thoughts, our affirmations, and our presence is threatening to the illusion of safety we get when we numb our spirits with the mundane, exhausting rituals of pursuing material success. Maybe life is just simpler and more palatable when we pour our vast imaginations into neat containers that do not leave space for the notion that there are things in the universe we cannot see and powers we cannot imagine. Whatever the reason I gave up my belief in magic, I remember that time as feeling utterly disconnected from the natural world. I remember my mindset as a teenager being like a gray expanse of space. I didn't believe my life had meaning or that the choices I made created ripples. It felt like we were all drifting, mindlessly consuming, and while I craved the magic that had illuminated my childhood, I was too afraid of what would happen if I opened that box of limitless possibility and dared to believe in mysterious things I could not see or touch. Most of all, I feared what would happen if I dared to believe in myself, that my presence had a purpose and a connection to the entire world.

For me, veganism has been a rediscovery of magic. One day, vaguely bothered by its title, I picked up a book titled *Eating Animals* that told me stories of cows bellowing for their babies and being artificially inseminated again, months later, to produce more babies, who were once again torn from their sides, because those babies were products to be sold for their parts. I learned the cows' milk that should have nourished their babies was instead pumped by the gallon from their bodies into plastic bottles, to be sold—perhaps on the same shelves that offered their babies' parts as "veal." I read about male chicks who are considered useless to the egg industry, mere by-products of the business of producing egg-laying hens, and how they are sent on their first day of life, chirping and blinking innocently, down a grisly conveyor belt right into the jaws of a macerator. I realized the chickens who lay eggs in battery cages for their entire miserable lives do not retire to sun-strewn sanctuaries in the countryside once their bodies have finished producing eggs but are instead killed and used for parts as well. I read about the toll factory farming takes on farmers, the physical injuries and mental degradation of slaughterhouse workers, and I realized all of this pain and suffering was being propped up down the line by people like me—people who were simply oblivious and hungry and too caught up in their lives to think about animals, but whose apathy is the greatest cause of animal abuse.

Reading that book, I understood I was connected to the slaughterhouse worker and the farmer and the chicken getting her throat slit, and that by making different choices I could quickly change my role in the story of animal exploitation. By going vegan, I became intentional about every single choice I made, and I learned everything I bought or wore or did had an undeniable weight to it and had the potential to negatively or positively affect others' lives. Food had purpose now, and power. Objects were imbued with meaning and significance and were often made in alternative ways by interesting artisans, rather than lifeless machines. For everything I ate or bought or used, I had to ask myself: "Where did this come from? What's it made from? Did anyone suffer for it?" It was overwhelming at first, but gradually I started to notice myself change in positive ways as a result of these intentional choices. My skin cleared up and the colds I'd gotten every few months for years completely vanished. These physical changes were welcome benefits—little thank-you notes from the universe for making ethical choices, if you will—but the most profoundly affecting change happened on a deeper level. There was something about living in a way that supported a world I wanted to create that gave me a feeling of inner alignment, of something within clicking into place. And there was something running through the people and the places and the businesses that prioritized animal rights and ethical practices, something about those who protect and advocate for the most vulnerable beings in society, something that felt warm and lovely and restorative and very much like that most healing magical force on earth—love.

Call it love, call it magic, call it what you will; my point is that we are all connected in some way by this energy that flows through every part of our lives: through our communications, through hugs, through the gifts we give each other and most definitely through the food we eat. It is possible— or rather, unavoidable—in every choice we make each day to impact other people and animals through those connective channels, to positively or negatively affect their lives. To me, that feels like a form of magic. And our bodies, the source of our magic, will be stronger and more powerful if they're not running off the fumes of the suffering of other sentient beings; if instead we choose to nourish them with delicious vegan food. As magical beings, we must remember that minding our magic

doesn't begin and end with abstaining from animal products—it's part of a larger responsibility to be good custodians of this planet, to cultivate a healthy synergy with our environment, as any good witch knows to do. We need to be conscious of the source of all the components that enhance our magic: crystals, chocolate, incense, etc. Veganism is not synonymous with perfection, though, and in a complex and wounded world where there is no such thing as perfection, it's left to us to fumble through and do our best. But veganism is a significant step toward creating a harmonious relationship with nature and utilizing the earth's resources mindfully. Hopefully, armed with the recipes in this book, you will see there is an abundance of amazing plant-based foods with which nature has gifted us that make this world an altogether more beautiful, more magical place.

I'm so proud that Imana, Tylor and my friends at The Protego Foundation have created this book to remind us why veganism is an essential branch of magic and explain how cultivating a balanced relationship with animals and the natural world—protecting, rather than exploiting our environment—can only enhance our powers as witches, wizards and magical people. *The Unofficial Harry Potter Vegan Cookbook* is filled with creativity, thoughtfulness and care, so I hope you'll brew yourself a warm beverage, sit down, relax and let all that energy in as you turn the pages. I hope you'll use this book to rediscover your own love of magic and, most especially, of the healing power of delicious plant-based food grown by mindful farming methods and prepared with loving hands.

—EVANNA LYNCH
The *Harry Potter* films' Luna Lovegood and creator of *The ChickPeeps* vegan podcast

Introduction

S FANS, WE LOOK TO our magical series as a form of escape—a world where our problems can be solved with just a wave of a wand or a quick conjuring of a potion. But we are taught early on in the *Harry Potter* series that we are capable of protecting those who are the most vulnerable not with the Elder Wand or the other Deathly Hallows but with a simple act of kindness or love.

Our goal with this cookbook full of plant-based recipes inspired by the wizarding world is to show how we can all choose kindness and love for the most vulnerable of creatures in our world whenever we sit down to eat. We can choose to conjure the strongest Shield Charm possible for our fragile planet by choosing plant-based foods. We can choose to live like Luna, Hermione, Hagrid and Newt, all of whom have taught us that every creature, no matter how big or small, is important and worthy of love.

It takes nothing to be kind, and now you don't have to miss out on feasting during those movie marathons! Charm your fellow Potterheads with vegan Peppermint Toads, Exploding Bonbons, and Cauldron Crisps. Our hope is that you can bewitch your friends and family with plant-based dishes that will Apparate you to the wizarding world like Bangers & Mash, Pumpkin Juice, and Treacle Tart. You can take the dishes featured in the pages of the *Harry Potter* series and bring their vegan versions to life in your own kitchen.

Whether you are a witch who has already been enjoying plant-based snacks as you study for your O.W.L.s or you're a warlock looking to defend the ones who may need your help the most, in the following pages you'll find the necessary step-by-step instructions, handy cooking tips and Kitchen Witch wisdom needed to whip up tasty wizarding dishes.

The strongest form of magic each of us has doesn't come from a wand—it comes from our ability to love.

—Tylor Starr

What Does Vegan Mean?

Learn how the foods you eat can change the world for the better.

VEGAN VS. PLANT-BASED

Many folks new to eating more plants and ditching animal products think the terms "vegan" and "plant-based" are interchangeable, but the two differ in many ways that may not always be apparent to those just starting out. Just like how "Squib" and "Muggle" both refer to someone who has no (or very little) magical ability, the terms also describe two very different situations for the communities they represent.

Plant-Based: Someone who considers their eating habits as plant-based eats a diet consisting mainly or entirely of plants—including fruits, vegetables, grains, legumes, seeds and nuts—and avoids eating animals in any form.

Vegan: As defined by The Vegan Society and coined in 1944, someone who is vegan follows a lifestyle and philosophy that seeks to exclude— as far as is possible and practicable—all forms of exploitation of, and to, animals used for food, clothing or any other purpose. Vegans eat the same as people who are plant-based, but extend their abstinence from animal exploitation to other aspects of their life that plant-based observers may not.

For example, someone who is vegan will not purchase shoes made out of cow skin, also known as leather; attend a show at SeaWorld or a circus that uses animals since animals used for entertainment is a form of "speciesism"; or use products tested on animals, since they believe testing on animals is a cruel, unkind and unscientific way to develop products.

For the purposes of this book, all recipes are considered vegan and plant-based since all of them use plants rather than animal products. Therefore, the terms can be used interchangeably.

WHICH INGREDIENTS ARE PLANT-BASED AND WHICH AREN'T?

Sometimes the hardest part of switching to a plant-based diet or a vegan lifestyle is figuring out which ingredients come from animals and which don't.

The switch from animal-derived ingredients and foods can be difficult, and the biggest piece of advice when starting on this journey is to remember that's what it is: a journey. Everyone has to start somewhere with that first step. Don't be too hard on yourself. Much like nobody is perfect at casting spells or brewing potions on their first day at Hogwarts (even Hermione turned herself into a cat-like creature once), this transformation takes time and patience. You won't get everything 100 percent correct right off the bat, but being kind to yourself and remembering why you are choosing to eat in a way that is better for your health, the planet and the billions of animals that call Earth home will keep you motivated as you continue down this path.

Vegans eat all of the same things you currently eat, just without the honey, eggs, milk and meat. One of the easiest tricks in determining if an ingredient is vegan is to stop and ask yourself, "Where did this ingredient come from and did it come from an animal?" For example, imagine you see something that has honey in it. Ask yourself, "Does honey come from an animal?" The answer, of course, is yes, since everyone knows honey is created by bees. So, because it comes from a bee, who only produces about 1/12th of a teaspoon of honey in their life before humans steal it for our tea and biscuits, honey is not vegan or plant-based.

The recipes in this book will be familiar to fans of *Harry Potter*, but instead of using eggs from hens, milk from mother cows and body parts from clever pigs, we use things like mushrooms, beans, coconut milk and so much more! For a complete list of vegan alternatives and our favorite plant-based brands around the world, see Magical Vegan Alternatives on pg. 12.

WHY DO PEOPLE CHOOSE TO GO VEGAN?

ANIMALS

What if you could take the creature-saving lessons in the *Harry Potter* books from characters like Hermione Granger, Luna Lovegood and Hagrid and apply them to your life? Someone who eats vegan for an entire year saves the lives of more than 100 animals, including shellfish, fish, chickens, turkeys, pigs, cows and other animals! Newt Scamander would be proud!

But why should not eating animals matter to someone? Haven't we always done this to animals? Continuing to do something simply because that's the way it's been done is a logical fallacy, which is sure to dock you some serious House points. As we know, in both the wizarding world and the non-magical world, prejudice against someone because of unimportant differences like magical ability, species, race, gender and more are not an excuse for oppression. To choose to eat animals is a form of something called "speciesism."

HEALTH

For those looking to improve their health, plant-based eating can be more effective than even a Pepperup Potion!

Plant-based foods are generally low in saturated fats, high in fiber, full of complex carbohydrates and other essential nutrients and are 100 percent cholesterol-free. The average vegan has a cholesterol level that is 77 points lower than the average meat-eater's. This is important for heart health because a landmark study found no heart attacks in people with a cholesterol level below 150—the average vegan's is 133. Plant-based foods also contain antioxidants, which fight inflammation and can counter carcinogens found in our bodies. Research has shown over and over again that vegans and people who eat a plant-based diet are between 25 and 50 percent less likely to get cancer than meat-eaters.

Incorporating more plants into your diet and leaving animal products off your plate will have you experiencing the health benefits millions of people around the world enjoy as part of their plant-based diet.

THE ENVIRONMENT

There is no denying our planet is experiencing a climate crisis that gets worse and worse every day. Every year, more and more of the Amazon rainforest is being cut down and burned to make more grazing land for cows who are going to be killed for meat. What would the wizarding world do if the Forbidden Forest was being cut down and burned to make room for cows to graze?

Researchers at the University of California, Riverside have calculated that cooking just one burger made of animal meat causes as much pollution as driving an 18-wheeler for 143 miles. Loma Linda University released a study that shows vegans have the smallest carbon footprint and generate a volume of 41 percent greenhouse gases less than meat-eaters. Clearly, only one of these diets is acting in favor of the planet. What kind of difference do you want to make?

Whether you are choosing to banish animal products from your plate and eat kindly for yourself, the animals or the planet, we hope you can delight in the magic of eating plant-based meals in these spellbinding recipes!

What Is Speciesism?

We would be remiss to create a book that ties the creature-saving messages of the *Harry Potter* series with the kindest way to eat and not mention why. The simple answer: fighting speciesism.

People for the Ethical Treatment of Animals (PETA), the authority on fighting speciesism, defines the term as "the human-held belief that all other animal species are inferior," and because of speciesist thinking, humans only consider animals—all of whom have their own desires, needs and complex lives—as means to human ends. Put bluntly, the idea that animals exist for humans to use for food, clothing, entertainment and experimentation is speciesist thinking.

In *Harry Potter and the Deathly Hallows*, the trio comes across a dragon who has been chained, beaten and abused down in the vaults of Gringotts bank. This dragon was forced to exist for no other reason than to be a form of security for the Gringotts Goblins; her bodily autonomy was taken away, rendering her incapable of making decisions on how to live her life in a way that is meaningful and important to her. We are taught in the book that this is wrong, that forcing a living creature into such a situation is speciesism.

If you clapped when Buckbeak was saved from execution, you understand fighting speciesism. If you cheered when that Ukrainian Ironbelly broke out of Gringotts and felt air on her face for the first time, you understand fighting speciesism. If you cried when Dobby or Hedwig were killed, you understand fighting speciesism.

Presenting vegan recipes for dishes inspired by the *Harry Potter* universe is a form of fighting speciesism, a form of magic that doesn't require a wand.

Magical Vegan Alternatives

Gathering plant-based foods may feel daunting at first,
but you might be surprised to find just how many delicious vegan ingredients
can be used in your all-time favorite recipes.

DAIRY

Butter/Margarine:
Coconut butter, avocado oil,
olive oil and coconut oil

Buttermilk: Nondairy milk of
choice with 2 tsp apple cider
vinegar or lemon juice

Condensed Milk: Oat-based
and coconut-based

Creamer: Coconut- or oat-
based creamer

Milk: Oat milk, almond
milk, pea milk, cashew milk,
coconut milk/evaporated
coconut milk, hazelnut milk,
rice milk, hemp seed milk,
pistachio milk, soy milk and
pecan milk

Sour Cream:
Thick vegan Greek yogurt, oat
fraiche, soy quark, vegan cream
cheese with a squirt of lemon
juice or cashew cheese

CHEESE

Vegan cheeses are made
without animal-based casein,
the protein that gives cheese its
signature gooey goodness. Here
are some of our favorite brands
of no-harm cheese (organized
by type). Each will delight your
taste buds and melt your heart.

Blue Cheese: Jay & Joy,
Follow Your Heart

Brie: Jay & Joy, Nuts For
Cheese, Wildbrine

Cheddar Cheese: Verdino,
Daiya, Violife

Cream Cheese: Oatly, Simply V,
Violife, Kite Hill, Daiya,
Tofutti

Feta: Violife, Follow Your Heart

Goat Cheese: Jay & Joy, Spero

Gouda: Violife,
Daiya Smoked Gouda-Style
Block

Mozzarella: Violife, Soyananda,
Mondarella, Daiya

Nutritional Yeast: BioToday,
Bragg

Parmesan: Violife,
Follow Your Heart

Vegan Shredded Cheese: Daiya,
Violife

Whipped Cream:
Overnight chilled can of
coconut milk. Only use the
cream from the top and whip
up until stiff peaks form.
Discard the water.

Yogurt:
Coconut yogurt, almond
yogurt, soy yogurt,
oat yogurt and cashew yogurt

EGGS

Egg Salad: Medium-firm and firm tofu

Fried Eggs: Rice flour batter and pumpkin, sweet potato or ackee (canned Jamaican fruit) yolk

Omelette, Quiche Filling and Frittata: Chickpea flour, mung bean flour

Scrambled Eggs: Silken tofu and medium-firm tofu (or mixed)

How to enhance egg flavors: Kala namak salt/ black salt is an important ingredient that replicates the eggy/sulfur taste in savory dishes like a chickpea omelet or scrambled tofu.

For Sweet Baking: Applesauce, ground flaxseeds, baking soda plus lemon or vinegar, silken tofu, overripe banana, aquafaba, ground chia seeds, cornstarch, nut butter or peanut butter

Aquafaba is the liquid brine from a can of chickpeas. It's a truly magical ingredient that whips up like a cloud. It is the perfect egg-white substitute when making meringues or fluffy cake batters.

For Savory Baking: Arrowroot powder, cornstarch, soy protein powder

For Savory Cooking: Chickpea flour, medium-firm tofu, mung bean flour, silken tofu

SEAFOOD

Crab: Hearts of palm, young jackfruit, artichokes

Lobster: Lobster mushrooms

Salmon: Marinated firm tofu with crispy nori

Scallops: King oyster mushrooms

Shrimp: Lion's mane mushrooms, king oyster mushrooms and hearts of palm

Smoked Salmon: Carrots

Tuna: Chickpeas (tuna flakes), jackfruit, marinated tomato, watermelon (sashimi/poke)

Whitefish: Banana blossom

How to enhance fishy flavors:

Nori sheets, wakame salad, kombu, vegan fish sauce, lemon, lime, samphire, tarragon, algae oil, purslane, chives, white miso paste, mirin, sushi vinegar, spirulina, vegan oyster sauce, parsley, vegan butter, white pepper, vegan white wine or white wine herb vinegar, garlic, vegan furikake

MEAT

Beef/Steak: Dehydrated lion's mane mushrooms, tofu.
All kinds of mushrooms (like king oyster) and tempeh are great for meat substitutes like beef, suitable for roasted or shredded beef. Use dry rubs and marinades to enhance the flavors and textures of your vegan meat options.

Canned Mock Chicken/Abalone Meat: Marinated vital wheat gluten

Chicken: Cauliflower, soy curls, oyster mushrooms

Chicken Fillets and Chunks: Medium-firm or smoked tofu, seitan, oyster mushrooms

Ground Beef/Minced Meat: Walnuts, chestnut mushrooms, lentils, pulled oats, soy mincemeat, minced aubergine

Ham: Glazed tofu, seitan roast

Pulled Pork: Young jackfruit in brine

Vegan bacon can be made from rice paper filled with marinated tofu or tempeh slices with a smoky glaze. For vegan bacon bits, try crispy coconut flakes.

SAUSAGE

White beans (lupini or cannellini) are the best main ingredient to make any kind of vegan sausage. Here are a few of my favorite brands based on sausage type.

Bratwurst and Sausage:
  Beyond Meat, Field Roast, Lightlife, Garden Gourmet and Future Farm

Breakfast Sausage:
  Beyond Meat, MorningStar Farms, Gardein and Garden Gourmet

Chorizo:
  Cacique Soy Chorizo, Simple Truth Meatless Chorizo, Garden Gourmet and Heura

How to enhance meat-y flavors: Liquid smoke, smoked paprika, soy sauce/tamari, Marmite, vegan red wine, onions, smoked garlic, balsamic vinegar, smoked sea salt and pepper, mushrooms in chili oil, chili crisp, spice blends, red miso paste, tomato paste, maple syrup, dark molasses, vegan Worcestershire sauce, mustard

NATURAL FOOD COLORING

If you would like to abstain from food coloring that is tested on animals, you can use...

Black: Activated charcoal

Blue: Blue spirulina, butterfly pea flower tea/powder

Green: Matcha, spinach (powder), spirulina

Lilac: Freeze-dried blueberries

Orange: Alphonso mango puree, carrot juice/powder

Pink: Freeze-dried raspberries, pink pitaya powder, strawberry puree/juice

Purple: Blackberry juice, butterfly pea flower tea with lemon added

Red: Beetroot powder or juice, cherries, pomegranate juice

Yellow: Ground turmeric, saffron

SWEETENERS

If you would like to abstain from sweeteners that contain bone char, you can use...

Agave syrup

Brown rice syrup

Brown sugar

Coconut sugar

Dark coconut syrup

Dark molasses

Dried prunes

Golden syrup: Lyle's

Korean corn syrup

Maple syrup

Medjool dates, date sugar or date syrup

No bee honey: BioToday

Organic granulated sugar (unbleached)

Pomegranate molasses

Treacle: Lyle's

Vegan condensed milk (oat- or coconut-based)

AGAR AGAR is a jelly-like ingredient derived from algae and a go-to gelatin substitute. Boil it to create vegan jellies, custards and puddings.

CHOCOLATE

If you would like to abstain from chocolates with dairy and sweeteners that are not cruelty free, you can use the following ingredients and brands...

Dark Chocolate:
  Lovechock

Milk Chocolate:
  Bonvita, iChoc and Mattisson

White Chocolate:
  Cacao butter, cashew butter and coconut butter

CONDIMENTS

Check out these cruelty-free sauces, dressings and marinades.

Almond Butter: Terrasana and BioToday

Balsamic, Red Wine and White Wine Vinegar: Mussini

Cashew Butter: Horizon

Chili Crisp: Lee Kum Kee

Coconut/Liquid Aminos: Yakso

Fish Sauce: Arche

Gojuchang (Fermented Korean Chili Paste): Haechandle

Hot Sauce: Flying Goose, McIlhenny

Kimchi: Pulmuone

Mayonnaise: Hellman's, Mister Kitchens, Jean Baton, Follow Your Heart

Oyster Sauce: Lee Kum Kee

Peanut Butter: Mister Kitchens and Whole Earth

Pesto: PuroVegan green and rosso

Sambal: ONOFF spices

Soy Sauce: Kikkoman

Sriracha Mayo: Flying Goose

Stem Ginger: Fi-Ji

Sweet Chili Sauce: Lima

Tahini: Sebahat

Trassi: Faja Lobi

White and Red Miso: Hikari

Worcestershire Sauce: Sanchon and Annie's

PREFERRED BRANDS

There are numerous vegan brands out there, but these are the ones the Kitchen Witch thinks are particularly spellbinding.

Beyond Meat

For the most realistic and juicy meat replacements, Beyond Meat is truly iconic. Delivers on flavor and has a positive impact on our planet.

Must Try: Beyond Burgers, sausages, meatballs and mince

Follow Your Heart

This brand has been making vegetarian and vegan products in the U.S. since 1970, beginning with their revolutionary egg-free mayo, Vegenaise.

Must Try: Vegenaise, ranch dressing and feta crumbles

Gardein

Getting its start in 2003, Gardein is the go-to brand for vegan meats and frozen snacks that are sure to have you racing back to the store for more.

Must Try: Chick'n Tenders, Turk'y Roast and F'sh Filets

MorningStar Farms

The go-to brand of meatless meat for Americans since it was founded in 1974. While not all of their products are vegan, the company has announced they will be phasing out eggs and milk in their products.

Must Try: Veggie Popcorn Chik'n, Veggie Chorizo Nacho Bites, Vegan Meat Lovers Burger

Violife

Violife comes from the Greek word "vios", which means life. This brand offers cheese for grating or shaving by the block, pre-grated melting cheeses and even cheeses specifically for grilling. Best of all, their cheeses are free from allergens (such as nuts) and GMOs.

Must Try: Halloumi, camembert, Greek white (feta), prosociano wedge (Parmesan) and cheddar slices

Kitchen Witch Tips

THE KITCHEN IS THE heart of the home—a constant source of energy to be exchanged between you and the food that will be shared with loved ones. As above, so below.

Invite magic into your kitchen with these witchy tools to create enchantment throughout your space. Use the freshest ingredients possible with the intent of mindfully enjoying your meals and turn the act of cooking into a sacred one.

A practicing Kitchen Witch takes everyday tools and creates a nurturing environment where these ingredients can flourish, grow and be transformed. The process of planning out a wonderful dish, the visualization of the food, gathering the ingredients and cooking the meal can feel like alchemy. A Kitchen Witch is enchanted and driven by the nourishment that food and plants provide. Cooking every meal is invoking a spell and performing a ritual. I always welcome the elements of fire, earth, water and air and let the brewing commence! Here are some other steps you should consider before you begin.

DECLUTTER AND CLEANSE THE KITCHEN BEFORE YOU START COOKING

Burn incense to cleanse your space and purify all cooking surfaces with Florida Water, a citrus-scented cologne first developed in the early 1800s and believed to have metaphysical cleansing properties. The best incense aromas for cleansing are cloves, dragon's blood and cedar. Open the windows to invite positive energy in return.

Don't want to smoke cleanse? Grab a few old pans and bang them together or hit a wooden spoon against the back of a cauldron or pan. The hard sounds will cleanse any stagnant energy that is not serving your kitchen. Having a wooden broomstick lying around the kitchen is always helpful to sweep away the energies you do not want to bring to the table. Cooking a meal requires both physical and spiritual attention. To a Kitchen Witch, the entire house is a sacred space, so be sure to bring this energy into all the areas of your home.

CREATE A MAGICAL ATMOSPHERE IN THE KITCHEN

Music is a great way to set the tone and mood for what you are going to cook, as the vibrations will run through the food. This gives so much soul to whatever you create. Each recipe in this cookbook has a selection from the music of *Harry Potter* as a pairing option to immerse you and anyone you're cooking with in the wizarding world while you whip up your meal. There's nothing more magical than baking Aunt Petunia's pudding to "Dobby the House Elf." Set the tone you want to have in your kitchen. Even meditation music or vibrational frequencies can be very relaxing and nourishing for the soul. Always cook with feeling.

MAKE ROOM FOR EASILY ACCESSIBLE DRIED SPICES

Save a space in your home for storing dried spices, then make the most of your herbs by properly storing them in labeled jars. Doing so will help you invoke the feeling that cooking is always a magical experience, just like potion-making in the dungeons of Hogwarts. Whether medicinal or simply delicious, every spice has a magical property. Make sure your spices retain their potency by storing them out of sunlight.

A few of my favorite spices to work with and their associated magical properties:

- **Bay leaves** to write and burn intentions
- **Cardamom** lust, clarity and warmth
- **Chili** passion
- **Cinnamon** fertility and protection
- **Cloves** banish negativity and promote healing
- **Ginger** power
- **Fennel seeds** confidence and courage
- **Star anise** good luck and protection

CREATE A SMALL KITCHEN ALTAR

Create a small space in which to build your kitchen altar. This can include a candle (for example, I love to use white or red candles), a photo of one of your ancestors to stay close to your culture and roots and a little cauldron to fill with whatever you desire, such as offerings. Make sure the altar is small and can be moved and cleansed easily. Treat the altar as a living, breathing hearth element of the kitchen.

TAKE GOOD CARE OF MAGICAL KITCHEN TOOLS

A wooden spoon is often seen as the Kitchen Witch's wand. Never put these in the dishwasher or wash them with soap! Treat with olive oil often and wash them with water. Use filtered water to prevent chalk from building up in the teapot for your special tea brews. To remove any chalk or hard water buildup, fill the pot with water and lots of vinegar and boil. Make sure to keep your knives sharp and pleasant to work with. Cast iron pans are some of my favorite pans to use when cooking. If treated well, you can use them forever. Never wash cast iron pans with soap, only water. After cooking, coat the inside of the pan with olive oil, rubbing well. Wash a mortar and pestle with water and oil frequently (never soap).

SOOTHE COOKING BURNS

Cooking accidents happen. Cool and soothe burns by using a cotton ball to apply aloe vera directly to the affected area. For further relief, add a little diluted essential oil, such as lavender or tea tree.

COOK WITH CRYSTALS

Love is the most important ingredient and vibration in the process of cooking, which is why I always have a big piece of rose quartz in a little corner of the kitchen. Nature provides love and all the tools that we need to survive and thrive. To amplify this energy, place rose quartz in your kitchen or tuck it into a pocket in your apron. It will make a difference and your dish will taste even better. Crystals that help with digestion are citrine, moss agate and fluorite. Fluorite is great for witches with stomach issues like IBS, who (like me!) reap great benefits from these magical crystals.

TREAT INGREDIENTS WITH MINDFUL INTENT

Bringing compassion to the table for vegans is vital. Treat every ingredient with care, taking into account the journey and lifespan of the plants you intend to use. Consider how long it took the tomato you're about to use to grow—perhaps it struggled but thrived against all odds. We should treat everything we consume with respect and waste nothing. Compost or recycle what you can. Set intentions for every time you step into the kitchen. For example: "May this food nourish me, heal me and provide me the nutrients I need for my mind, body and soul." Or, "May this food comfort me against sadness or feeling deprived, may this food lift my spirits up to invoke more hope, positive energy and joy." Always give thanks for what you are about to eat, then enjoy the fruits of your labor.

AWAKEN THE SENSES AND ENJOY THE PROCESS

Cooking is magic. Opening the senses to the process will connect you to the cooking experience. Note the smell of the spices as they sizzle in hot oil, the aroma of fresh citrus as you cut into a lemon, the sounds of ingredients simmering away in a pot. Focus on each step that is happening and it will deepen your appreciation for what cooking does to your spirit. You will eat and digest the food with more manifested intention. Everything we consume will be stored in our memories forever, making each dining experience extraordinary.

AVOID MICROWAVES FOR MAGICAL COOKING

Ovens literally transform your ingredients with their warmth. Microwaves, on the other hand, are never my preferred option, as I believe they take away the magic you enchanted and created with your ingredients. The stove and oven are the heart elements of the kitchen.

MAKE A BOTTLE OF MOON WATER TO COMPLEMENT YOUR MAGICAL COOKING

There are four elements that are used during cooking: water, air, earth and fire. Water is a vital part of the process of cooking and enchanted/amplified moon water will enhance the magic you create in the kitchen. To create moon water, cleanse a bottle and fill it with filtered water. Set your intentions, then leave it out at night in the moonlight. Collect it before the sun rises the next morning and you're all set. Use moon water to cook with, brew teas, cleanse the kitchen or enchant your magical kitchen tools. You can make moon water every day, not only by the full moon (but it should be noted that this is when it's the most potent).

TREAT YOURSELF TO A KITCHEN WITCH ORACLE DECK

To connect more to herbs, spices and the meaning of each ingredient, an oracle deck based on Kitchen Witchery will help you build more insight into how these ingredients can benefit you daily. Perform readings on which herb you need to have in your life right now. Which herb can help you overcome certain health issues? Each herb or spice holds an element and energy to help you on your magical cooking journey.

USE THE BEST QUALITY SALT YOU CAN FIND

A very important ingredient with innumerable magical purposes, salt binds all cooking together. There are plenty of varieties to choose from, such as Himalayan salt, smoked salt, kala namak salt, sea salt and so much more. Salt is the earth element, directly from the sea, and will make every dish you cook come alive. High quality salt attracts love, blessings and cleansing in the heart of the home.

ALWAYS TASTE DURING THE COOKING EXPERIENCE

When you are in the middle of the process of cooking, take a moment to taste test. See where the flavors are taking you. What needs to be adjusted? Ask yourself: "Do I need to add more salt or acid, or do I need to play with the heat more to caramelize or roast an ingredient?" Use your senses and your intuition to give the dish what it needs. That is where the magic happens.

My favorite plants to have on the kitchen counter:

Aloe vera Good for burns and homemade hair and skin masks, the gel is incredibly moisturizing

Basil Amazing in pasta sauces, dressings and elixirs

Chives Great herb to finish soups, salads and sandwiches

Mint To brew tea and infuse in desserts, breakfasts, juices and smoothies

Rosemary For rustic stews, gravies and roasted vegetables

Thyme Amazing to flavor breads and add to teas

Modern Kitchen Witch Tools/Equipment:

High-speed blender

Food processor

Slow juicer

Dutch oven

Spatula

Silicone baking mat instead of parchment paper to reduce waste

Stand mixer/electric mixer

Small and medium saucepans

NOTE: Uncommon equipment such as the gemstone mold used in the Diadem Gemstone Gummies recipe on pg. 118 are available from many online retailers.

Classic Castle
Steamed Porridge,
pg. 28

Magical Mornings

Draw back the curtains on your four-poster bed and head down the moving staircases for a tasty plant-based breakfast before class. Whether you have a long day of helping unicorns in the forest or double Potions class down in the dungeons, these magical morning treats are sure to keep you satisfied.

Featuring vegan twists on classic dishes like bacon and eggs and grab-and-go breakfast treats like Cheery Owl Donuts and Rock Cakes to take with you on the way to your first flying lesson, your mornings just got a whole lot more magical.

What are you waiting for? Class is about to begin and you don't want to get on the Transfiguration professor's bad side on the first day!

Bacon and Eggs Three Ways

When Harry is tasked with cooking breakfast on Dudley's birthday in *Sorcerer's Stone*, the day has barely begun and he already wishes it would end. But even the most basic of breakfast staples can be transformed into something wondrous with the right ingredients (in this case, coconut yogurt, pea milk and perfectly seasoned tofu).

PREP TIME 10 minutes **COOK TIME** 45 minutes **YIELD** Enough for 4 bad relatives

INGREDIENTS

FRIED EGGS

Vegan Egg Yolk

- ½ cup (80 g) sweet potato, cubed
- 1 Tbsp (15 ml) extra-virgin olive oil
- 2 tsp (4 g) nutritional yeast
- ¼ cup (60 ml) water
- 1 Tbsp (10 g) cornstarch
- 1 Tbsp (15 ml) coconut milk
- ⅔ tsp (3 g) kala namak salt
  Pinch of black pepper, optional

Vegan Egg Whites

- ¼ cup (60 ml) coconut yogurt
- ¼ cup (60 ml) pea milk
- ¼ cup (31 g) rice flour
- ¼ tsp (0.5 g) sea salt

RICE PAPER BACON

- 4 rice paper sheets
- ½ cup (125 g) medium-firm tofu

RICE PAPER BACON MARINADE

- 3 drops liquid smoke
- 2 Tbsp (30 ml) soy sauce
- 2 cloves of garlic
- 2 Tbsp (30 ml) vegan butter, melted
- 1 Tbsp (15 ml) olive oil
- 1 tsp (2 g) smoked paprika
- 1 Tbsp (20 g) maple syrup
- 1 tsp (5 ml) tomato paste
- 1 tsp (1 g) red chile flakes

OMELET

- 1 cup plus 3 Tbsp (150 g) chickpea flour
- ½ cup (125 g) silken tofu
- ½ cup (125 ml) cold water
- ¼ cup (50 ml) oat milk
  Salt and pepper to taste
- ⅔ tsp (3 g) kala namak salt, optional
- 1 tsp (2 g) onion powder

- 1 tsp (2 g) garlic powder
- ½ tsp (1 g) smoked paprika
- 2 Tbsp (5 g) nutritional yeast

SCRAMBLED EGGS

- 1 cup (250 g) medium-firm tofu
- 1 Tbsp (10 g) curry powder
- 4 cloves of garlic
- 2 tsp (4 g) mixed dried Italian herbs
- ¼ tsp (0.5 g) kala namak salt
  Pinch of black pepper
- ¼ tsp (0.5 g) ground nutmeg
- ¼ cup (65 ml) oat cream
- ¼ cup (22 g) shredded vegan cheese
- 1 Tbsp (13 g) vegan butter, melted
- 2 Tbsp (20 g) fresh chives, chopped

MAGICAL METHOD

1. Fill a small saucepan with water.

2. Boil the sweet potato until soft, approximately 10 minutes. Meanwhile, mix the other vegan egg yolk ingredients in a small mixing bowl. Set aside until the potato is cooked.

3. Mash the sweet potato and let it cool for a few minutes before adding to the yolk mixture. Mix well until smooth and creamy.

4. In a small saucepan on medium-high, add the yolk mixture and whisk constantly for about 4 minutes. Set aside to cool down before frying up the vegan fried eggs.

5. Preheat oven to 400 degrees F (200 degrees C). Line a baking sheet with paper or mat. Using scissors, cut strips of rice paper that are two fingers thick.

6. Mix all rice paper bacon marinade ingredients together. Crumble the tofu and add ⅓ cup of the marinade. Brush the rice paper sheets with the remaining marinade. Lay half the sheets on the baking sheet. Crumble the tofu over each and sandwich with another sheet of rice paper.

7. Bake the rice paper bacon

until golden and crispy, 14 to 16 minutes. Flip halfway through. When it's cooked, let it crisp up and cool at the same time, about 10 minutes.

8. Meanwhile, make the vegan omelet. Add all the dry ingredients to a bowl and mix until there are no lumps. Transfer mixture to a blender, add the wet ingredients and blend until batter is smooth.

9. Melt butter in a cast iron pan and let it get foamy. Pour in the omelet batter and turn the heat on medium-low. Cook 5 minutes on each side. Set aside until serving time.

10. Meanwhile, prepare the vegan egg white batter. In a small mixing bowl, add dry ingredients followed by wet. Mix until smooth and put in the fridge until ready to use.

11. Prepare the scrambled eggs. Add a small amount of olive oil or vegan butter to the pan. Crumble in the tofu (make sure the liquid is squeezed out) in chunks and cook for 2 minutes. Add the spices and fry off until fragrant. Add the oat cream and vegan cheese. Mix until melted and combined.

12. Finish the scrambled tofu with the melted vegan butter,

chives and an extra crack of black pepper.

13. In a frying pan, add a shot of olive oil, then add 2 generous Tbsp of vegan egg white batter. Fry on medium-low for 3 to 5 minutes. Cover with lid.

14. Add a dollop of the vegan yolk mixture in the middle, spread it out evenly and cover with lid for another 30 seconds. Serve immediately with freshly squeezed orange juice, toast, fresh-baked bread and vegan butter.

....

The Kitchen Witch is humming...
"Harry's Wondrous World"—John Williams

....

From the Kitchen Witch

Crack a little bit more black pepper onto your food if you are surrounded by negative relatives. Black pepper is often used in banishment and protection spells. Use the peppercorn as a magical charm and you'll banish hunger with pepper seeds.

Cheery Owl Breakfast Donuts

It's a cold, rainy morning in the Great Hall and you're desperate for something tasty to prepare you for the spell and charm studies to come. Suddenly, a brown barn owl flies overhead and drops off these gorgeously baked donuts with cheery owl cereal on top—a dusting added just before finishing in the oven to maximize its aromatics. They're so delicious, they make you wonder what magic the day may bring.

PREP TIME 15 minutes **COOK TIME** 35 minutes **YIELD** 7–8 donuts

INGREDIENTS

DONUTS

- ½ Tbsp (7.5 ml) lemon juice
- 1 cup (250 ml) almond milk
- ½ cup (90 g) plain, sugar-free cornflakes
- ½ cup (90 g) coconut sugar
- 1¼ cup (150 g) self-raising flour
- Pinch of sea salt
- 1 tsp (2 g) ground cinnamon or gingerbread spices
- 2 Tbsp (30 ml) vegan butter, melted
- 2 Tbsp (30 ml) unsweetened apple sauce
- 1 tsp (5 ml) vanilla extract
- 1 Tbsp (15 g) stem ginger, sliced
- Zest of 1 lemon

GLAZE

- 1⅛ cups (290 g) white almond butter
- 1 tsp (5 ml) vanilla extract
- ½ cup (170 g) agave syrup
- 1 tsp (2 g) ground cinnamon
- Zest of 1 lime

TOPPINGS

- Cereal of choice

MAGICAL METHOD

1. Combine the lemon juice and half the almond milk and cornflakes. Let soak for 15 minutes.

2. Strain the milk and set aside. Push the soaked cereal through the sieve well so all the flavor packs in the milk and batter. Discard the soaked cereal.

3. In a large mixing bowl, add the dry ingredients, except the ground cinnamon or gingerbread spices. Make a small well in the center and add the cereal milk, wet ingredients and remaining cornflakes and almond milk.

4. Using a spatula, mix well. When the batter is smooth and combined, add the ground cinnamon or gingerbread spices.

5. Add some melted butter or coconut oil in the donut mold so the donuts do not stick.

6. Pour in the batter, filling up ⅓ of the way (do not overfill).

7. Bake for 20 to 25 minutes at 355 degrees F (180 degrees C) or until golden brown.

8. Mix the glaze ingredients, then dip the cooled donuts in the glaze.

9. Sprinkle your cereal of choice over the donuts before serving.

The Kitchen Witch is humming…
"Hogwarts Forever! and the Moving Stairs"
—John Williams

Classic Castle Steamed Porridge

A bright and early morning is shining through the stained glass in the Great Hall. The four long House tables are laden with tureens of porridge, fruit plates and mountains of toast beneath the enchanted ceiling. The perfect school morning has arrived, and this porridge will ensure hunger is held at bay through practice on your broom over the pitch.

PREP TIME 5 minutes   COOK TIME 20 minutes   YIELD Enough for 4 witches and wizards

INGREDIENTS

PORRIDGE

2½ cups (600 ml) almond milk
1 Tbsp (10 g) loose-leaf Earl Grey tea
1 tsp (2 g) culinary lavender
Zest and juice of 1 lemon
2 cardamom pods
1 tsp (2 g) Chinese 13 spices
1 tsp (2 g) gingerbread spices
1 tsp (5 ml) vanilla extract
¼ tsp (1.5 ml) rose water
2 tsp (2 g) cinnamon powder
1 cinnamon stick
1½ cups (77 g) rolled oats
Half a Pink Lady or Braeburn apple, grated
Pinch of salt
¼ cup (60 g) maple syrup

TOPPINGS

Blueberries
Strawberry slices
Peanut butter
Raspberries
Banana slices
Hemp seeds
Chia seeds
Dried cranberries
Green or golden kiwi slices
1 or 2 passion fruits

MAGICAL METHOD

1. In a medium-size saucepan, add almond milk, Earl Grey, lavender, lemon zest, cardamom, Chinese 13 spices, gingerbread spices, vanilla, rose water and cinnamon powder and stick. Let everything infuse for at least 10 minutes.

2. Strain the milk through a sieve and pour back into the pan. Add the rolled oats and stir until combined.

3. Add grated apple and lemon juice. Mix in with the steaming oats. Let the mixture steam on low heat for 6 to 8 minutes.

4. Mix in a pinch of salt and the maple syrup.

5. Garnish with your favorite fruits and toppings and serve immediately.

The Kitchen Witch is humming…
"Hogwarts Forever! and the Moving Stairs"—John Williams

From the Kitchen Witch

A tiny sprinkle of lavender on an early school morning is a belly hug for long hours of relaxed learning and a soothed mind.

Merpeople Breakfast Bowl

As Harry finds his way through the weeds of the Great lake
in *Goblet of Fire*, a siren song leads him to an underwater secret:
a merpeople colony on the lake floor, complete with underwater gardens,
stone dwellings and art. It's easy to imagine them tucking into this refreshing
fruit bowl, big enough to hold a cardamom and coconut feast.

PREP TIME 5 minutes COOK TIME 15 minutes YIELD Enough for 2 merpeople

INGREDIENTS

NICE CREAM

- 2 mangoes
- 4 bananas
- 1 tsp (5 ml) vanilla extract
- ¼ cup (50 ml) coconut milk
- ⅔ tsp (0.5 g) ground cardamom
  Zest and juice of 1 lime
- 1 Tbsp (10 g) blue spirulina powder
- ½ cup (125 ml) coconut yogurt

MERMAID TAILS (OPTIONAL)

- ¼ cup (80 g) vegan marzipan
- 1 tsp (4 g) blue spirulina
- 1 tsp (4 g) matcha powder, diluted with a drop of water

TOPPINGS

- ½ cup (90 g) puffed spelt
- 1 cup (85 g) fresh coconut chunks
- ½ cup (65 g) mixed tropical fruits: pineapple, papaya and mango
- ¼ cup (36 g) almonds
- ¼ cup (40 g) dried kiwi, cubed
- ¼ cup (40 g) freeze-dried pineapple
- ¼ cup (40 g) banana chips
- 1 Tbsp (20 g) hemp seeds
- 2 Tbsp (32 g) white almond butter
- 1½ Tbsp (12 g) coconut flakes
- 1 Tbsp (10 g) nata de coco

MAGICAL METHOD

1. The night before, dice the bananas and mangoes. Make sure the chunks are small to make it easier for your blender. Divide them separately on a tray and freeze.

2. To make the optional mermaid tails, press the marzipan into a silicone tail mold. Turn the mold upside down and push the tail out on a flat surface. Make the edges neat and dye them with spirulina and matcha if you choose.

3. Add the frozen fruit to your blender with vanilla, coconut milk, cardamom and lime zest and juice.

4. Blend on medium-high until it forms a sorbet-like texture.

5. Scrape and divide the nice cream mixture between two bowls. Color one of them with blue spirulina.

6. Place a scoop of each nice cream into each bowl. Swirl the coconut yogurt through. Sprinkle with toppings of choice and mermaid tails. Serve immediately.

....

The Kitchen Witch is humming...
"Underwater Secrets"— *Patrick Doyle*

....

From the Kitchen Witch

Blue spirulina, a superfood that can help combat fatigue and improve digestive health, is the magical cherry on top of this breakfast bowl.

Bath Buns

When Harry and Ron visit Hagrid's hut in *Prisoner of Azkaban*, the half-giant serves them tea and a plate of bath buns—a generous gesture, but his cooking isn't appetizing by a long shot. This batch, however, with their dainty pearl-sugared tops and shiny finish, are guaranteed to be gone in a flash.

PREP TIME 10 minutes **COOK TIME** 25 minutes **PROOF TIME** 2 hours **YIELD** 8 bath buns

INGREDIENTS

BUNS

½ cup (125 ml) oat milk

3 Tbsp (30 g) coconut sugar

1 Tbsp (12 g) dried yeast or 2 Tbsp (24 g) fresh yeast

1¾ cups (225 g) strong white bread flour

1 tsp (2 g) ground cinnamon
Zest of 1 orange

1 tsp (2 g) ground ginger

1 Tbsp (10 g) caraway seeds

¼ tsp (2 g) salt

1 cup (227 g) vegan butter, room temperature, plus 2 Tbsp (28 g) vegan butter, melted

1 tsp (5 ml) vanilla extract

COATING

1 Tbsp (20 g) maple syrup

½ cup (125 ml) oat milk

GARNISH

2 Tbsp (20 g) sugar pearl candy

1 Tbsp (10 g) caraway seeds

MAGICAL METHOD

1. Warm the oat milk to body temperature. In a bowl, mix with coconut sugar and yeast until combined. Set aside for 10 minutes. The mixture should be bubbly after 10 minutes, which means the yeast is alive and well.

2. Add the dry ingredients to a mixing bowl.

3. Cut the butter into small chunks and add to the dry ingredients. Mix on low speed. If mixing by hand, rub the butter between your fingers until you get a sand-like texture.

4. Add the vanilla extract, then gradually add the yeasty milk mixture to make the dough.

5. When the dough forms, set mixer on medium to high speed and knead for 10 more minutes. Do not be alarmed if the dough appears very wet—it's supposed to be. Don't be tempted to add more flour. If kneading by hand, knead with passion and put all of your good intentions into it. The dough should spring back a little when you poke it with your finger.

6. Add 2 Tbsp of melted vegan butter into the mixing bowl. Cover with a damp tea towel and let rest in a warm place. Let the dough proof for 1½ hours.

7. Meanwhile, add maple syrup and oat milk to a small bowl and mix until combined. Set aside.

8. For the garnish, add the sugar pearl candy and caraway seeds to a small bowl. Crush them a bit with the back of a spoon. Set aside.

9. Knead the dough into a long sausage shape. Cut into six pieces.

10. Roll each piece individually, shape them to your liking and tuck in the bottoms of the buns.

11. Lay them on a baking sheet lined with baking paper. Make sure you have enough space between them or they'll come out as hot cross buns. Cover with a damp tea towel and let the buns proof for another 30 minutes.

12. Preheat the oven to 375 degrees F (190 degrees C).

13. After proofing, brush on the maple milk and sprinkle on the garnish.

14. Bake for 15 to 20 minutes until golden brown and fluffy. Serve with your favorite jam, vegan butter and a glorious cup of tea.

....

The Kitchen Witch is humming…

"Reunion of Friends" —John Williams

....

Rock Cakes

In *Sorcerer's Stone*, Hagrid welcomes Harry and Ron to his hut with a plate of "shapeless lumps with raisins," nearly hard enough to break your teeth. Hagrid's guests are polite enough to pretend to enjoy the offerings, but these baked goods will only elicit heartfelt gratitude with every bite.

PREP TIME 5 minutes **COOK TIME** 35 minutes **YIELD** 10–12 rock cakes

INGREDIENTS

- 3 cups (375 g) all-purpose flour
- ½ cup (100 g) coconut sugar
- 1 tsp (2 g) gingerbread spices
- ¼ tsp (1 g) salt
- ½ cup (125 g) vegan butter, cold
- 1 tsp (5 ml) vanilla extract
- Zest of 1 orange
- ⅓ cup (73 g) dried apricots, chopped
- ⅓ cup (50 g) raisins
- 2½ Tbsp (25 g) dried cranberries
- 1 Tbsp (15 ml) apple sauce
- ½ cup (125 ml) almond milk

MAGICAL METHOD

1. Preheat oven to 400 degrees F (200 degrees C). Line a baking sheet with paper or a mat and set aside.

2. In a large mixing bowl, mix the flour, sugar, gingerbread spices and salt.

3. Chop the cold butter into small chunks and rub them between your fingers into the dry ingredients. It should end up looking like wet sand.

4. Add the vanilla extract and orange zest and mix until combined.

5. Mix in the dried fruits and apple sauce.

6. Add the almond milk to combine into a rough dough. Do not overmix. You want to end up with short and crisp cakes.

7. Divide the dough into 12 balls of equal size and push them down slightly on the lined baking sheet.

8. Brush the cakes with almond milk and sprinkle with a little bit of coconut sugar.

9. Bake for 20 to 25 minutes until crispy and golden brown. Serve slightly cooled with vegan butter, homemade jam and a hot cup of tea.

....

The Kitchen Witch is humming…
"The Norwegian Ridgeback and a Change of Season"
—*John Williams*

....

Buckbeak's Stuffed
Pumpkins, pg. 52

Spellbinding Starters

T he first-years have been Sorted and the headmaster has announced his start-of-term notices. It's now time for the feast to commence with some scrumptious vegan starters that would tide over even the biggest of giants (to say nothing of half-giants).

You'll exclaim, "This is just like magic!" when you dig into these plant-based versions of bouillabaisse (a dish beloved by French witches and wizards), scallops that will transport you to the depths of the sea and a hearty pea soup—just make sure you eat it before it eats you!

Now tuck in, avoid eye contact with the Bloody Baron and enjoy the start of another magical year—and another magical meal.

Dutch Split Pea Soup

When a shrunken head warns you about the pea soup at the Leaky Cauldron, much as Harry learns in the film adaptation of *Prisoner of Azkaban*, you'd better be ready to eat it before it eats you. Fortunately, this thick, cruelty-free soup is not only tame—it's bound to make any gloomy day more enjoyable.

PREP TIME 10 minutes **COOK TIME** 2 hours **YIELD** Enough for 4 magical friends

INGREDIENTS

1 whole leek, sliced into rings, thoroughly washed
2 medium carrots, thinly sliced
1 white onion, finely diced
3 sticks celery, thinly sliced
2 cups (280 g) diced celeriac
2 cups (280 g) diced waxed potatoes, unpeeled
Olive oil or vegan butter
1 sprig rosemary
2 sprigs thyme
1 tsp (2 g) fennel seeds
2 tsp (4 g) caraway seeds
½ tsp (1 g) ground cloves
1 tsp (2 g) ground nutmeg
2 bay leaves
5 cloves of garlic, crushed
2 drops liquid smoke
1 Tbsp (10 g) white miso paste
1 Tbsp (10 g) Dijon mustard
2 cups (400 g) dried green split peas
8¾ cups (2 L) vegetable stock
1 Tbsp (2.5 g) nutritional yeast
Salt and freshly cracked black pepper to taste
Juice of 1 lemon

GARNISH

Vegan rookworst (Dutch smoked sausage) or substitute a really smoky plant-based sausage
Vegan katenspek (Dutch deli slices) or vegan bacon rashers
Vegan bacon bits (see Bacon and Eggs Three Ways on pg. 22, then crumble the strips)
Celery leaves

MAGICAL METHOD

1. In a large pot over medium heat, add a shot of olive oil or vegan butter. Fry the leeks, carrots, onion, celery, celeriac and potatoes with a pinch of salt and pepper until onion is translucent, about 7 to 8 minutes.

2. Add the rosemary, thyme, fennel seeds, caraway seeds, cloves, nutmeg, bay leaves, garlic and liquid smoke. Stir until combined and fragrant.

3. Add the miso paste and mustard, then mix until fully incorporated.

4. Add the split peas and stock. Bring to a boil, then reduce heat, cover with lid and let toil and trouble (read: simmer) for 1 hour.

5. After 1 hour, see if the pieces of

the peas have broken down. If not, let simmer for another 15 to 30 minutes or until fully cooked. The peas should be fully incorporated into the broth.

6. Season with nutritional yeast plus salt, pepper and lemon juice to taste.

7. Add the rookworst and cook until warmed through. If using smoky plant-based sausages, fry them in a frying pan until cooked, then slice into bite-size pieces before adding to the soup.

8. Garnish the soup with vegan katenspek, crispy bacon bits and celery leaves. Serve with buttered rye bread.

....

The Kitchen Witch is humming…
"Diagon Alley and the Gringotts Vault"
—John Williams

....

From the Kitchen Witch

There, there, dry your tears. If chopping onions is too much, darling, wet a cloth with cold water and put between the cutting board and onions. Your stinging, weeping eyes will soon be cleared up.

Aromatic Bouillabaisse

In *Goblet of Fire*, foreign visitors arrive flying over the castle, making their grand entrance with graceful, mystical elegance. In order to welcome the Beauxbatons students and make them feel at home, the cauldrons in the kitchens have been boiling and dancing for hours. A warm belly hug from the aromatic broth and wonderful pairings make for a magnifique début to the new term. "Excuse me, are you wanting ze bouillabaisse?"

PREP TIME 15 minutes **COOK TIME** 1½ hours **YIELD** Enough for 4 foreign visitors

INGREDIENTS

BROTH

- 8¾ cups (2 L) water
- 1 Tbsp (10 g) miso paste
- Peel of 1 orange
- ¼ cup (10 g) dried seaweed
- 1 onion, roughly chopped
- 3 celery sticks, roughly chopped
- 2 medium carrots, roughly chopped
- 3 cloves of garlic, roughly chopped
- 2 bay leaves
- Half a lemon
- 1 star anise
- ½ cup (35 g) fennel stalks
- 1 Tbsp (16 g) tomato paste
- 1 piece kombu
- 2 sprigs thyme

- 1 sprig rosemary
- 10 black peppercorns
- 1 tsp (2 g) freshly grated nutmeg
- 4 saffron threads

VEGAN CRAB

- 2 cups (400 g) hearts of palm

VEGETABLES

- 1 carrot
- 2 king oyster mushrooms, sliced
- 1 cup (71 g) fennel bulb, sliced
- 1 leek, root and dark green tops removed and discarded, chopped

VEGAN SALMON

- ½ cup (125 g) medium-firm tofu

- 1 Tbsp (10 g) Old Bay Seasoning, divided
- Salt and pepper to taste
- ½ cup (125 ml) fresh carrot juice
- 1 tsp (2 g) garlic powder
- ½ Tbsp (7.5 ml) soy sauce
- 2 cloves of garlic

CRISPY SALMON SKIN

- 1 Tbsp (8 g) rice flour
- 1 Tbsp (15 ml) cold water
- 2 rice paper sheets
- 2 nori sheets

VEGAN SHRIMP

- 2 cups (400 g) vegan shrimp
- Salt and pepper to taste
- ½ cup (125 ml) vegan white wine or lemon juice

Parsley, chopped

1 Tbsp (14 g) vegan butter

GARNISH

Fennel fronds

Lime slices

Chives, chopped

MAGICAL METHOD

1. In a cauldron over medium heat, add all broth ingredients except saffron. Let the broth come to a boil. Stir vigorously. Reduce the heat, cover with lid and let simmer for 45 minutes to 1 hour.

2. Remove the lid and let the broth simmer for 15 minutes.

3. Place the saffron in a small bowl. Add 1 Tbsp (15 g) of lukewarm water to the saffron and let it sit for 5 minutes. Add the saffron and water to the broth.

4. Adjust the seasoning to your liking. More umami? Add miso paste. More tang? Add lemon juice or just a pinch of salt. Be careful with miso paste—it is naturally salty. Keep the broth on low heat while you season to taste.

5. Add the hearts of palm (vegan crab) to the cauldron to infuse and cook with the broth for 10 minutes.

6. Remove to a plate.

7. Peel and chop the carrot into half-moons and add to broth.

8. In a frying pan over medium heat, add a shot of olive oil and fry the mushrooms. Season with salt, pepper and a bit of lemon juice and fry until golden brown. Add to the broth.

9. Fry the fennel bulb and leeks on medium heat until translucent, about 5 minutes, then season to taste with salt and pepper. Add to the broth.

10. Stir, taste and season if needed.

11. Squeeze all of the moisture out of the tofu. Cut the tofu into "fishy squares," then cut diagonal lines all over to let the flavors seep in. Season vigorously with ½ Tbsp (5 g) Old Bay Seasoning, salt and pepper. Rub in well.

12. In a small bowl, combine the remaining ½ Tbsp (5 g) Old Bay Seasoning, carrot juice, garlic powder, soy sauce, salt and pepper and let sit for at least 1 hour.

13. Meanwhile, start the crispy salmon skin. Make a paste with the rice flour and water and mix until combined.

14. Cut up the rice paper and nori in the same shape as the tofu pieces.

15. To make the skin, layer the nori sheets on top of the tofu pieces. Next, wet the rice paper sheets on both sides and stick to the nori layer.

16. Fry the tofu pieces (skin side down first) in a frying pan with 1 Tbsp olive oil for 3 to 4 minutes on medium heat.

17. Finely slice the hearts of palm and add to pan.

18. Crush the 2 cloves of garlic and add them to the pan. Mix until combined. Season with salt and pepper.

19. If there is space in your pan, fry your vegan shrimp alongside the other vegan seafood. Otherwise, grab another pan and fry until golden brown on all sides for 5 minutes on medium heat. Season with salt and pepper and deglaze the pan with white wine or lemon juice.

20. Add chopped parsley and 1 Tbsp vegan butter and mix until combined. Set all the vegan seafood aside until serving.

21. Remove the lemon half from the broth.

22. When serving this soup, place the vegan seafood in the middle of each bowl, then ladle in the broth. Garnish with fennel fronds, slices of lime and chopped chives.

....

The Kitchen Witch is humming…

"Foreign Visitors Arrive"

—Patrick Doyle

From the Kitchen Witch

Serve this wonderful soup alongside a crispy baguette with salted vegan butter on the side, a squeeze of lemon and a glass of white wine. Nice and light and better zan ze heavy castle food.

Savory Lakeside Scallops

The home of Hogwarts's giant squid, the Great Lake holds its share of secrets, including a colony of merpeople that Harry encounters in *Goblet of Fire*. Who's to say what other rare and wonderful creatures lurk in its depths? It's a question worth pondering while standing on the shore as you tuck into these mushroom-based scallops.

PREP TIME 10 minutes COOK TIME 25 minutes YIELD Enough for 2 hungry merpeople

INGREDIENTS

BROTH

- 2 cups (500 ml) vegetable stock or leftover bouillabaisse broth (see Aromatic Bouillabaisse on pg. 40)
- 2 cloves of garlic
- ½ cup (125 ml) vegan white wine
- 1 nori sheet
  Half a lemon
- 1 cup (42 g) kombu
- 1 spring onion
- 2 tsp (4 g) fennel seeds
- 1 Tbsp (15 ml) light soy sauce
- 2 Tbsp (30 ml) mirin seasoning
  Salt and pepper to taste

SCALLOPS

- 6 king oyster mushrooms
- ½ cup (100 g) vegan butter, plus more for the sauce
  Freshly cracked black pepper
  Zest and juice of 1 lemon
- 1 Tbsp capers

GARNISH

Microgreens
Lemon slices

MAGICAL METHOD

1. In a large saucepan on medium heat, add all the broth ingredients and let come to a boil.

2. Meanwhile, slice the mushroom stalks (vegan scallops) into scallop-shaped pieces two fingers thick. Save the tops of the mushrooms for another recipe. Using a knife, score the mushroom tops to create a fun chessboard effect. Add the mushrooms to the broth and let cook for 10 to 15 minutes until chewy and springy.

3. Remove the mushrooms and dab them dry with paper towels.

4. In a frying pan on medium-low heat, melt the vegan butter until it foams up. Add the mushrooms scored-side down and fry for 4 to 5 minutes or until golden brown and crispy.

5. Remove the mushrooms from the pan and add one ladle of the broth. Cook for 10 to 15 minutes to reduce to a glossy and sticky sauce.

6. Add a bit of vegan butter, freshly cracked black pepper, zest and juice of 1 lemon and 1 Tbsp capers. Stir until combined.

7. Serve the scallops with the sauce on the side. Garnish with microgreens and lemon slices and enjoy immediately.

SERVING TIP: Serve the scallops with pan-fried samphire or a cold wakame salad.

The Kitchen Witch is humming…
"The Black Lake" —Patrick Doyle

From the Kitchen Witch

Serve these fleshy vegan scallops as they are, with a sweet pea puree or topped with crispy vegan bacon. The variations are as endless as the lake is deep.

Rabbit Food Grazing Board

When Dudley has to go on a diet in *Goblet of Fire*, his typical treats (chunky chocolate chip cookies, fizzy drinks, knickerbocker glories and bacon sandwiches) are swapped out for lighter fare, much like this sampler of crispy crudites, delectable fruits and a refreshing tzatziki. He might not enjoy it, but you certainly will.

PREP TIME 20 minutes **ASSEMBLY TIME** 10 minutes **YIELD** Enough for 4 bad relatives

INGREDIENTS

- 2 cups (300 g) olives
  Seeds of 1 pomegranate
- 2 Tbsp (7.5 g) chopped parsley
- 4 pieces whole grain pita bread
- 2 cups (240 g) celery, sliced into bite-size sticks
- 2 cups (256 g) baby carrots, halved
- 2 cups (300 g) cherry tomatoes
- 1 cucumber, sliced
- 2 cups (300 g) mini peppers
- 1¼ cups (140 g) seedy crackers
- 2 cups (230 g) mixed nuts (almonds, cashews, hazelnuts, etc.)
- 2 cups (300 g) red and green grapes

VEGAN TZATZIKI

- 3 cups (750 ml) coconut yogurt
- 4 cloves of garlic
- 1 Tbsp (20 g) maple syrup
  Zest and juice of 1 lemon
- 1 tsp (2 g) dried mint
- 1 tsp (2 g) ground cumin
- 1 Tbsp (15 ml) extra-virgin olive oil
- ¼ cup (20 g) fresh dill, chopped
- ¼ cup (20 g) fresh mint leaves, chopped
  Salt and pepper to taste
- ½ cucumber

MAGICAL METHOD

1. In a grilling pan on medium-high heat, add the olives and grill on each side until grill lines appear. Place the olives in a small serving dish on top of the serving board. Garnish with pomegranate seeds and parsley.

2. Toast the pita until crispy, then chop into triangles and place on the serving board.

3. Place the veggies, crackers, mixed nuts and grapes on the serving board.

4. In a small mixing bowl, add the vegan tzatziki ingredients except the cucumber and mix until well combined.

5. Grate the cucumber over a clean tea towel, then wrap up the towel to squeeze out the excess moisture.

6. Add the cucumber to the tzatziki and mix well. Serve in a small dish.

The Kitchen Witch is humming…
"Prologue: Book II and the Escape From the Dursleys" —John Williams

From the Kitchen Witch

Nourishing body, mind and soul is a self-love practice. While slicing up the fruit and vegetables, set an intention for what these foods should give you. Food is healing.

Great Lake Diving Dip

A meal inspired by the spirit of the water, informed by the vitamin- and nutrient-rich weeds that thrive in its murky depths, this hearty dish bursting with leafy greens hails straight from the bottom of the lake, a delicacy of the horned green creatures that call it home.

PREP TIME 5 minutes   COOK TIME 10 minutes   YIELD Enough for 4 water demons

INGREDIENTS

- 1 **cup (85 g) wakame**
- 1 **tsp (5 ml) sesame oil**
- 2 **cups (60 g) spinach**
- 6 **cloves of garlic**
  Salt and pepper to taste
- 1 **cup (250 g) vegan cream cheese**
  Zest and juice of 1 lemon
- ⅔ **cup (150 g) vegan sour cream or yogurt**
- ½ **cup (80 g) chopped artichokes in oil**
- ¼ **cup (32 g) fresh coriander, chopped**
- 2 **Tbsp (20 g) capers**
- 2 **spring onions**
- 1 **avocado**
- ⅓ **cup (42 g) fresh dill, chopped**

SERVING OPTIONS

- **(Seaweed) crisps or crackers**
- **Baguette**
- **Cucumber sticks**
- **Crispy nori snacks**

MAGICAL METHOD

1. In a bowl, soak the wakame in hot water for 15 to 20 minutes. (If using fresh wakame, skip this step.)

2. In a small saucepan, add sesame oil and saute the spinach until wilted, about 1 to 2 minutes. Add the garlic and let cook for 2 minutes. Season to taste with salt and pepper. Let cool completely.

3. In a food processor, add the wakame, garlic spinach, cream cheese, lemon zest and juice, sour cream, artichokes, coriander, capers, spring onions, avocado and dill, then blend until silky smooth.

4. Season to taste and serve with your favorite dippers.

The Kitchen Witch is humming…
"Golden Egg" —Patrick Doyle

From the Kitchen Witch

This seaweed diving dip is best served chilled for extra refreshment on hot summer days.

Great Lake Tempura

While enjoying a sunny afternoon sitting near the lake, you notice a series
of magical aquatic plants growing along the waterfront, just waiting to be harvested
and turned into a feast of crispy vegetable fritters. Tucking into this delectable,
lightly fried dish will feel like a reward for all that exam prep.

PREP TIME 10 minutes   **ASSEMBLY TIME** 35 minutes   **YIELD** Enough for 4 hungry Merpeople

INGREDIENTS
VEGETABLE VARIETY

- ½ eggplant
- ½ zucchini
- 1 cup (50 g) asparagus tips
- 10 slices lotus root
- 1 cup (100 g) bamboo shoots
- 2 cups (250 g) green beans
- 1 cup (120 g) samphire
- 2 cups (130 g) enoki mushrooms
- 1 tsp (1 g) sea salt

BATTER

- ¾ cup (100 g) all-purpose flour
- ¾ cup (100 g) rice flour
- 1¼ cups (300 ml) ice-cold sparkling water
- 2 Tbsp (30 ml) vegan mayo
- Zest of 1 lime

DIPPING SAUCE

- ½ cup vegan mayo (123 g)
- Zest and juice of 1 lime
- 1 tsp (5 ml) sriracha

ADDITIONAL INGREDIENTS

- 6 cups (1.5 L) deep-frying oil
- Limes or lemons to garnish
- Sesame seeds to garnish

MAGICAL METHOD

1. Cut the vegetables as you like: rings, vertical slices or "diagonalley," just make sure the pieces are roughly the same size so they cook evenly.

2. Dry the vegetables with a cloth.

3. To prepare the tempura batter, add the dry ingredients and mix with a whisk.

4. Slowly whisk in the sparkling water. Note: Do not overwork the batter—it is totally fine to have some lumps.

5. Refrigerate batter for 15 minutes.

6. Mix the three dipping sauce ingredients in a serving bowl.

7. Preheat oil to 350 degrees F (180 degrees C).

8. Dunk the vegetables in the batter one by one. Tap off the excess batter against the side of the bowl.

9. Fry until golden and crispy. Turn them over so they cook evenly. Remove to a towel-covered plate to drain the extra oil.

10. Sprinkle with sea salt immediately after frying (this keeps the tempura crispy). Or, put it into the oven to keep it hot and crispy. Garnish and serve straight away with the dipping sauce.

....

The Kitchen Witch is humming...
"Golden Egg" —Patrick Doyle
....

From the Kitchen Witch

For extra flavorful tempura, swap out the sparkling water with your favorite beer!

Buckbeak's Stuffed Pumpkins

A very proud creature stands guard just a few steps away.
The best way to approach, as Harry learns in *Prisoner of Azkaban,* is to
make a graceful bow. From there, grab what you'll need for this recipe,
a roasted fall favorite perfect for the season of the witch.

PREP TIME 10 minutes   **COOK TIME** 45 minutes   **YIELD** Enough for 4 friendly visitors

INGREDIENTS

- 4 mini pumpkins
- 1 onion, finely diced
- 2 cups (150 g) shiitake mushrooms, sliced
- 1 cup (75 g) chestnut mushrooms, sliced
- ½ cup (80 g) wild rice, washed and drained
- 1 cup (250 ml) mushroom stock
- 6 cloves of garlic
- 2 sprigs thyme, shredded and finely chopped
- 1 sprig rosemary, shredded and finely chopped
- 4 fresh sage leaves, shredded and finely chopped
- 1 tsp (5.5 g) tomato paste
- 1 tsp (5 g) Marmite
- ½ tsp (1 g) ground cinnamon
- 1 cup (150 g) pecans
- 1 cup (30 g) spinach
  Zest of 1 orange
- ½ cup (60 g) dried cranberries
- ⅓ cup (80 g) vegan feta
- ½ cup (30 g) chopped parsley
  Salt and cracked black pepper to taste
- 1 tsp lemon juice to taste

MAGICAL METHOD

1. Carefully cut off the tops of the pumpkins, then scoop out the pulp and seeds. (Note: Wash the seeds and bake at 375 degrees F [180 degrees C] for 20 minutes for an easy snack. Sprinkle with sea salt after baking.)

2. Brush the pumpkins inside and out with olive oil and sprinkle with salt and pepper. Bake for 15 to 20 minutes.

3. In a medium pan on medium-high heat, add a shot of olive oil and fry the onion until glossy for about 6 to 8 minutes. Add a pinch of salt.

4. Add the mushrooms to the onions along with a pinch of salt and pepper. Seasoning at every stage will leave you with more depth of flavor at the end. Fry the mushrooms on medium-high heat until golden brown and caramelized.

5. Add the rice to a small saucepan on medium-low heat along with the stock. Cook for 8 minutes or until fluffy.

6. Back to the stuffing: crush the garlic into the mushrooms and cook until fragrant.

7. Add the thyme, rosemary, and sage to the lovely mushrooms. Your hut will smell phenomenal!

8. Add the tomato paste and cook, stirring constantly, for 2 to 3 minutes. Add the Marmite and ground cinnamon and stir until combined.

9. Add the pecans and spinach and cook until spinach is wilted, about 2 minutes.

10. Add in the cooked wild rice, orange zest and dried cranberries and mix until combined.

11. Crumble in the vegan feta and sprinkle the chopped parsley. Add salt, pepper and lemon juice to taste.

12. Scoop the filling into the mini pumpkins and put the tops back on. Bake at 355 degrees F (180 degrees C) for 5 minutes to infuse and mingle. Serve immediately.

....

The Kitchen Witch is humming…
"Saving Buckbeak" —John Williams

....

From the Kitchen Witch

Serve with a wonderful endive/arugula salad or enjoy as they are.
A magical way to start all your autumnal festivities.

Cunning Green Crudité Board

As Harry and Ron learn while disguised as Crabbe and Goyle in *Chamber of Secrets*, the emerald-green common room in the dungeons is the perfect setting for shooting dice or making plans with resourceful (and perhaps too cunning for their own good) housemates. The dungeon windows offer a view of the realm beneath the lake, as well as passing glimpses of the giant squid that calls it home. You may as well nosh on these cleverly presented green treats, served on a marble board as cold as the Head of House.

PREP TIME 2 hours to overnight **ASSEMBLY TIME** 10 minutes **YIELD** Enough for 4 Housemates

INGREDIENTS

TOFU FETA

- 1 cup (200 g) medium-firm tofu
- 1 cup (250 ml) extra-virgin olive oil
- Juice of 1 lemon
- 1 tsp (2 g) red pepper flakes
- 4 cloves of garlic
- 1 tsp (4 g) nutritional yeast
- 3 tsp (6 g) Italian dried herb mix (oregano, thyme and rosemary)
- 1 tsp (2 g) salt and pepper

ROASTED PADRÓN PEPPERS

- ¾ cup (150 g) Padrón peppers
- 1 Tbsp (15 ml) olive oil
- Salt and pepper to taste
- 1 lime

GREEN HUMMUS

- 1 tsp (2 g) baking soda
- Salt and pepper to taste
- 2 cups (400 g) chickpeas
- 1 cup (180 g) frozen peas
- ¼ cup (112 g) tahini
- ¼ cup (50 ml) extra-virgin olive oil
- ½ cup (120 ml) ice water
- 6 cloves of garlic
- ¼ cup (45 g) chopped mint
- ¼ cup (45 g) chopped coriander
- ¼ cup (45 g) chopped dill
- Zest and juice of 1 lime
- 2 tsp (4 g) cumin
- 1 tsp (2 g) sumac
- 1 tsp (2 g) ras el hanout, ground
- 1 tsp (5 ml) sesame oil

BASIL PESTO

- 5 cups (75 g) basil
- ½ cup (50 g) roasted pine nuts
- ½ cup (125 ml) extra-virgin olive oil
- 3 Tbsp (30 g) vegan Parmesan, shredded vegan cheese or nutritional yeast
- Juice of half a lemon
- Salt and pepper to taste
- 3 cloves of garlic

CRUDITÉ BOARD

- Green grapes
- 1 Granny Smith apple, sliced
- Pistachio nuts
- Green olives
- Edamame
- Dried kiwi
- Cucumber sticks
- 1 pear, sliced
- Marinated artichokes
- Seaweed crisps
- Zucchini chips

MAGICAL METHOD

1. Using a clean towel, press all of the excess moisture out of the tofu and pat dry. Cut into feta cubes and set aside.

2. Fill a glass jar with olive oil, lemon juice, red pepper flakes, garlic, nutritional yeast, Italian dried herb mix, salt and pepper. Mix until combined. Add the tofu pieces and let marinate for at least 2 hours, best overnight.

3. Rub Padrón peppers with olive

oil and salt and pepper to taste. Place on a grill or in a frying pan to blacken, grilling on both sides for 3 minutes until soft. Finish off with some extra salt and a sprinkle of lime juice. Set aside.

4. Fill a large saucepan with water and let it come to a boil. Sprinkle in baking soda and salt. Once the water is boiling again, add the chickpeas and peas. Let boil for about 5 to 7 minutes. The skin should become soft and easy to remove.

5. Let the chickpeas and peas cool slightly but not all the way. The hummus becomes silky smooth when the peas are still warm.

6. Add the rest of the hummus ingredients together with the chickpeas and peas to a food processor or blender. Blend until smooth. Adjust the seasoning to taste.

7. To make the basil pesto, add in all pesto ingredients to the clean food processor. Pulse to your desired texture. Season to taste.

8. Spoon the hummus and pesto into two bowls and place them in the middle of the board. Arrange the tofu feta, Padrón peppers and other charcuterie board ingredients as you desire and serve immediately.

....

The Kitchen Witch is humming…
"Cakes for Crabbe and Goyle"
—John Williams

....

Greenhouse Harvest Quiche

Picture yourself walking down a path to the greenhouses much as Harry does in *Sorcerer's Stone,* where you then pick the most beautiful herbs and vegetables. Now imagine a crispy and flaky tart, filled with fresh umami flavor and garnished with edible flowers. From root to tip and in between, this tart wants to be seen.

PREP TIME 15 minutes **COOK TIME** 45 minutes **YIELD** Enough for 6 Herbology students

INGREDIENTS

QUICHE

- 1 roll vegan puff pastry
- 1 medium carrot, peeled into ribbons
- 1 zucchini, peeled into ribbons
- 1 cup (75 g) variety of mushrooms
- ½ cup (35 g) green asparagus, sliced
- ¼ cup (30 g) bread crumbs

FILLING

- 1 cup (200 g) roasted paprika hummus
- ¼ cup (22 g) shredded vegan cheese
- 3 Tbsp (30 g) sundried tomato pesto
- ½ cup (125 g) medium-firm tofu
- 5 cloves of garlic, crushed
  Zest of 1 lemon
- ½ cup (120 g) oat crème fraîche or vegan cream cheese
- 1 tsp (5 ml) Dijon mustard
- 2 tsp (4 g) dried Italian herbs
- 1 tsp (2 g) smoked paprika
- 2 sprigs fresh thyme
- 1 sprig fresh rosemary, finely diced
- 1 tsp (2 g) ground nutmeg
  Salt and pepper to taste
  Small drop truffle oil, optional

GARNISH

Edible flowers (e.g., violets or chamomile) and fresh herbs (tarragon, parsley or basil)

MAGICAL METHOD

1. Preheat oven to 400 degrees F (200 degrees C).

2. Brush a tart tin with vegan butter. Be sure to get it in every nook and cranny of the tin so nothing will stick to the sides or bottom.

3. Line tin with puff pastry. Push in the sides gently. Trim any excess pastry hanging over the tin with a butter knife. Take the excess you have trimmed off and tuck it into the empty nooks and crannies.

4. Lay a 12-inch (30-cm) circle of baking paper on top of the tart tin. Fill the tin up with baking beans and press down gently. Bake in the oven for 20 minutes until the pastry is cooked but not browned.

5. Remove the baking paper and beans. Let the pastry cool for about 10 minutes.

6. Season carrot and zucchini

salt, pepper and olive oil and set aside. In a small frying pan with 1 Tbsp (15 ml) olive oil on medium to high heat, fry the mushrooms and asparagus for 3 to 4 minutes. Season with salt and pepper.

7. In a large mixing bowl, mix filling ingredients with a spatula until combined.

8. Sprinkle the breadcrumbs over the tart.

9. Layer the filling into the tart tin, then roll up each ribbon of zucchini and carrot and place it on top of the filling. Repeat until you are left with a beautiful rosy tart. Press the mushrooms and asparagus into the filling. Bake until golden brown and crispy, about 30 to 35 minutes.

10. Garnish and serve with a beautiful salad or bubbly drink.

....

The Kitchen Witch is humming…
"The Chamber of Secrets"
—John Williams

....

From the Kitchen Witch

Working with puff pastry affords you numerous options. You can make this tart in any shape or size you want. For example, mini versions to serve at a greenhouse party or picnic are highly enjoyable.

Dragon Roasted Nuts,
pg. 62

Mystical Munchies

As you and your friends sit through yet another boring magical history lesson, your mind wanders to the delicious food being sold at the snow-capped village down the road. But what are you to do if they don't have any vegan options when you visit this weekend?

No need for a spell or potion—these mystical munchies have you covered for your visit and beyond. Keep cool on those sunny afternoons at the pitch with Ice Cream Parlor Frozen Treats, crunch away on Dragon Roasted Nuts and even share some plant-based treats with your three-headed canine companion.

So enjoy yourself! Just don't forget your essay on the radical troll rights movement of the 1990s is due on Thursday!

Peppermint Toads

First mentioned in *Prisoner of Azkaban*, this delightfully minty, amphibian-shaped treat will linger on your palate long after you've hopped off to your next class. Don't be surprised if your lust for travel grows with every bite.

PREP TIME 5 minutes   COOK TIME 25 minutes   YIELD 6 peppermint toads

INGREDIENTS

PEPPERMINT FILLING
- ⅛ cup (25 g) vegan butter, room temperature
- 2 Tbsp (16 g) fresh mint, finely chopped
- ¼ tsp (1 ml) vanilla extract
- Zest of 1 lime
- ⅓ cup (75 g) white marzipan

TOADS
- 1½ cups (200 g) vegan white chocolate, finely chopped, divided
- 3–4 drops peppermint extract, to taste

GARNISH
- Edible ice blue luster dust
- Edible pearl white luster dust

MAGICAL METHOD

1. Fill about ⅓ of a medium-sized saucepan with water, then place a heat-proof well-fitting bowl on top (make sure it's a snug fit, because if any water hits the chocolate in the bowl, it will burn and become gritty).

2. Meanwhile, in a small mixing bowl, add the butter, mint and vanilla extract. Mix until combined.

3. Add the lime zest and marzipan and mix to form a thick filling. Refrigerate.

4. On medium-low heat, melt 1 cup (132 g) of the white chocolate for about 6 to 8 minutes and set the other ½ cup (68 g) aside. Be careful—if so much as one drop of water falls into the mixture, it will curdle.

5. Take the bowl off the pan and heat. Stir in the peppermint extract and remaining chocolate to melt in the residual heat, about 5 minutes.

6. Pour the chocolate onto a marble platter. Using a spatula, smear and guide the chocolate over the marble to cool it down. This technique will ensure a shiny finish on the toads and that the chocolate snaps a bit when you bite into it. When the surface of the chocolate becomes shiny, scrape down all the chocolate and pour it into a bowl.

7. Fill ¼ of the toad mold with white chocolate. Next, add ½ tsp (3 g) of filling, then end with more white chocolate. The chocolate should completely cover the filling. Tap the filled mold a few times on the counter to release any air bubbles.

8. Refrigerate for 25 minutes.

9. Tap the toads out of their molds, then coat with a dusting of luster dust. Enjoy right away.

....

The Kitchen Witch is humming...
"The Story Continues" —Patrick Doyle
....

From the Kitchen Witch

If you have leftover toads, heat up 1 cup and 2 Tbsp (280 ml) of your plant-based milk of choice and melt one or two toads to enjoy as a hot beverage.

Dragon Roasted Nuts

As seen in the film adaptation of *Half-Blood Prince,* these crackling roasted nuts make the perfect snack for just about any journey (no magical vending machine required). When opening the hot paper bag, a welcoming waft of smoke and chile flakes warms your spirit and lifts your mood. Just don't spoil your dinner!

PREP TIME 5 minutes   COOK TIME 50 minutes   YIELD Enough for 4 magical friends to go nuts with

INGREDIENTS

 2 cups (300 g) almonds, peeled
 2 cups (300 g) pecans
 2 cups (300 g) hazelnuts, peeled
 2 cups (300 g) peanuts
 1 tsp (2 g) sea salt
 2 tsp (4 g) chile flakes
 1 tsp (2 g) smoked paprika
 2 drops liquid smoke
 ½ cup (120 g) maple syrup
 ½ tsp (1 g) ground cinnamon
 1 tsp (2 g) garlic powder
 1 tsp (2 g) onion powder
 1 tsp (2 g) dried mango powder
 1 tsp (2 g) ground cumin
 1 Tbsp (15 ml) walnut oil
 1 Tbsp (15 ml) sesame oil
 1 tsp (2 g) dark muscovado sugar
 ½ tsp (1 g) allspice

MAGICAL METHOD

1. Preheat oven to 250 degrees F (120 degrees C).

2. Line a baking sheet with parchment paper and place the nuts on the parchment paper. Set aside.

3. In a small mixing bowl, mix remaining ingredients until combined.

4. Pour this mixture over the nuts and mix and coat well. Roast the nuts for 50 minutes, low and slow.

5. Let cool completely before enjoying immediately, bagging them for an on-the-go snack or giving to a magical friend.

The Kitchen Witch is humming…
"Harry Sees Dragons" —*Patrick Doyle*

From the Kitchen Witch

Hang a few dried chiles above your stove in the kitchen—the fiery vibrations absorb negative energy and will bring more deliciousness to your food (and life!).

Ice Cream Parlor Frozen Treats

There is nothing more satisfying after a day full of snagging new robes, telescopes and potion bottles in Diagon Alley than enjoying a glorious ice cream cone, much as Harry does in *Chamber of Secrets*. With light citrus notes of bergamot and a dash of lavender, the dairy-free Earl Grey ice cream makes for a refreshing treat, while the Strawberry and Peanut Butter blend boasts more than a cup of whipped coconut cream, making it a rich, sumptuous take on dairy-free dessert.

PREP TIME 10 minutes   COOK TIME 1 hour 30 minutes per batch   YIELD Enough for 6–8 strolling witches or wizards

EARL GREY AND LAVENDER

INGREDIENTS

- 1¾ cups (425 ml) evaporated coconut milk
- ½ cup plus 1 Tbsp (100 g) granulated sugar
- 3 Tbsp (20 g) loose-leaf Earl Grey tea
- Pinch of sea salt
- 1 Tbsp (10 g) culinary lavender
- 1 vanilla pod
- ¼ cup (55 g) cacao butter
- 2 tsp (10 ml) coconut oil
- Zest of 1 lemon
- 2 Tbsp (20 g) fresh blueberries, chopped

GARNISH

Lavender, lemon zest and vegan wafers

MAGICAL METHOD

1. In a small saucepan on medium, heat the milk to 175 degrees F (80 degrees C), about 4 to 5 minutes.

2. Add the sugar, Earl Grey, salt and lavender to the milk. Mix until the sugar is dissolved and let steep for about 10 minutes.

3. Pour the mixture through a sieve so you are left with the beautiful, sweet infusion of milk.

4. Slice the vanilla pod down the middle, scrape out the seeds and add the seeds to the milk. Add the cacao butter and coconut oil and let mixture cool completely.

5. Add the lemon zest and blueberries. Refrigerate for 1 hour before adding it to your ice cream machine or freezer. Stir every 30 minutes, and after 4 hours, you can scoop away. If using an ice cream machine, churn for 1 hour for a soft serve.

6. Serve in crispy ice cream cones or sundae glasses.

STRAWBERRY AND PEANUT BUTTER

INGREDIENTS

- ½ cup (76 g) strawberries, halved, stems removed
- 1 Tbsp (20 g) maple syrup
- 1 tsp (2 g) ground cinnamon
- ⅛ tsp (0.5 g) cream of tartar
- ¼ cup (50 ml) coconut milk
- 1 vanilla pod
- 1⅓ cups (325 ml) whipped coconut cream
- 1 can condensed coconut milk (1 cup [226 g])
- Pinch of sea salt
- ⅓ cup (80 g) salted caramel peanut butter
- Zest of 1 lime

GARNISH

Fresh strawberry slices, crushed peanuts and vegan wafers

MAGICAL METHOD

1. Preheat oven to 430 degrees F (220 degrees C). Line a baking sheet with parchment paper.

2. Place the strawberries on the baking sheet. Drizzle with maple syrup and sprinkle with cinnamon, then roast for 25 minutes. Let the strawberries completely cool before adding them to the ice cream.

3. Mix the cream of tartar into the coconut milk and set aside. Slice the vanilla pod down the middle, scrape out the seeds, add the seeds to the coconut cream and whip until soft peaks form. Add the condensed coconut milk and mix until combined. Add a pinch of salt and mix again.

4. Chop up the roasted strawberries and fold them into the ice cream base along with the peanut butter to create a ripple effect. Do not mix in completely. Transfer the ice cream base to a container and refrigerate for 1 hour.

5. Transfer to the ice cream machine and churn for 1 hour or put in the freezer for at least 4 hours and stir every 30 minutes for a silky smooth finish.

....

The Kitchen Witch is humming…
"Diagon Alley and the Gringotts Vault"
—*John Williams*

....

Coconut Snow Cones

It's the night of the winter soiree. In *Goblet of Fire*, the Great Hall
is decked out in silver and ice, much like these whimsical chilled refreshments,
the ideal way to cool off after dancing till dawn.

PREP TIME 10 minutes **COOK TIME** 20 minutes **FREEZER TIME** 4 hours to overnight
YIELD Enough for 4 waltzing witches or wizards

INGREDIENTS

SNOW CONE BASE

- 2 cups (480 ml) coconut water
- ½ cup (125 ml) condensed coconut milk

COCONUT SNOW/GRANITA

- 2 Tbsp (12 g) coconut flakes
- 1 can coconut milk
- ¼ cup (50 ml) coconut water
- Zest and juice of 1 lime
- 3 Tbsp (45 ml) coconut syrup
- ¼ tsp (0.5 g) coconut extract
- Small pinch of sea salt

GARNISH

- 1 tsp (2 g) coconut flakes each
- 2 Tbsp (20 g) nata de coco each
- Edible silver glitter

MAGICAL METHOD

1. For the crushed ice, fill an ice cube tray with coconut water and freeze overnight.

2. Start the granita. In a frying pan on low heat, add the coconut flakes and toast for 3 to 5 minutes.

3. In a large mixing bowl, add the toasted coconut flakes and the remaining granita ingredients. Mix until well combined.

4. Pour the granita into a freezer-safe container without a lid and freeze for 4 hours or overnight.

5. Stir well after 2 hours of freezing so the "snow" starts to form. When serving, drag a fork through the coconut mixture until snow forms. Or, add the mixture to your blender and crush into beautiful snow.

6. Start the assembly: Crush the coconut ice cubes either in a blender or by wrapping in a clean tea towel and bashing on the counter.

7. Fill the bottom of each cone with this crushed ice.

8. Pour some of the half cup of condensed coconut milk in the cone and top with the granita. Garnish each cone with coconut flakes, nata de coco and glitter.

....

The Kitchen Witch is humming...
"Neville's Waltz"—Patrick Doyle

....

From the Kitchen Witch

For a fruity touch, add a little bit of mango puree or raspberry to ripple and marble through the snow cones.

"No Fish" and Chips

First mentioned in *Sorcerer's Stone*, the Leaky Cauldron is a traditional pub, the sort of place you could easily imagine tucking into a platter of golden fried "fish" and a bounty of crispy chips, along with a tangy and creamy dipping sauce. Better get it while it's hot.

PREP TIME 10 minutes   COOK TIME 45 minutes   YIELD Enough for 2 hungry witches or wizards

INGREDIENTS

CHIPS

- 6 cups (1.25 L) deep-frying oil
  Salt to taste
- 5 cups (1 kg) unpeeled waxed potatoes, cut into thick fries

MUSHY PEAS

- 2 cups (300 g) frozen peas
- 2 Tbsp (30 ml) vegan butter, melted
  Zest and juice of 1 lemon
- ¼ cup (40 g) fresh mint, chopped
- ½ tsp (1 g) ground or freshly grated nutmeg
  Salt and pepper to taste

"NO FISH"

- 2 cans banana blossom in brine
- 1 tsp (2 g) Old Bay Seasoning
- 1 nori sheet, crushed
- 1 tsp (2 g) lemon zest and juice
- 6 cups (1.25 L) deep-frying oil
  Salt and pepper to taste

GINGER BEER BATTER

- ⅓ cup and 1 Tbsp (50 g) all-purpose flour
- ⅓ cup and 1 Tbsp (50 g) cornstarch
  Salt and pepper to taste
- ¾ cup (175 ml) cold ginger beer

TARTAR SAUCE

- 5 Tbsp (75 ml) vegan mayo
- ½ cup (125 ml) coconut yogurt
- 6 pickles, finely diced
- 2 Tbsp (20 g) fresh dill, chopped
- 1 tsp (5 ml) Dijon mustard
- 1 Tbsp (10 g) capers, chopped
  Zest and juice of 1 lemon
- 1 tsp (5 ml) pickle juice
  Salt and pepper to taste

GARNISH

  Lemon slices
  Parsley, chopped

MAGICAL METHOD

1. Preheat the deep-frying oil to 300 degrees F (150 degrees C).

2. Lay the fries on a tray, dry them off with a tea towel, lower them into the oil and cook for 5 minutes. After the first fry, scoop the fries onto a plate with a kitchen towel to drain the excess oil.

3. Heat up 2 cups (500 ml) water in a small saucepan. Bring to a boil and add the peas. Cook for 2 minutes, then drain and set aside.

4. In a food processor or blender, add the peas, melted butter, lemon zest and juice, mint, nutmeg, salt and pepper. Pulse four or five times if you prefer a chunkier texture; otherwise blend until smooth. Set aside until serving.

5. Drain the banana blossoms from the brine and wash with cold water. Take the biggest outer leaves, grab some of the fleshy parts, put them in the middle and roll the leaves up into a parcel. Dry with paper towel and season with Old Bay Seasoning, nori and lemon zest and juice, rubbing in well. Set aside.

6. In a large mixing bowl, add the batter ingredients, except the ginger beer. Make a well in the center and pour in the ginger beer. Whisk until the mixture comes together, about 30 seconds to 1 minute, being careful not to overmix. Refrigerate until needed.

7. Heat 6 cups (1 L) deep-frying oil to 355 degrees F (180 degrees C).

8. Drag the seasoned banana blossom pieces through the batter. Tap off excess batter and lower carefully into the oil, then fry for 2 to 3 minutes on each side until golden brown and crispy on all sides. Remove from oil and place on a plate with a kitchen towel to drain the excess oil. Season with salt and pepper.

9. Mix all the tartar sauce ingredients until combined.

10. Fry off the chips until golden and crispy for 4 minutes. Sprinkle with salt.

11. Squeeze the lemon slices, garnish with parsley and serve immediately with ice-cold ginger beer.

....

The Kitchen Witch is humming...
"The Knight Bus" —*John Williams*
....

69

Cauldron Crisps

A tornado of crispy, crunchy goodness coated with sweet spice, twisted and spiraled out of control in the bubbling, toiling oil, these enchanted spuds on a stick are a rare delicacy that make a big impression. They pair perfectly with a good book and a self-refilling beer.

PREP TIME 20 minutes   **COOK TIME** 1 hour   **YIELD** Enough for 4 adventurous guests

INGREDIENTS

CRISPS
- 6 cups (1.25 L) deep-frying oil
- 4 large unpeeled waxed potatoes

SEASONING
- 1 tsp (2 g) smoked paprika
- 1 tsp (2 g) ras el hanout
- 1 tsp (2 g) garlic powder
- 1 tsp (2 g) dried onion powder
- 1 tsp (2 g) dried rosemary
- 1 tsp (2 g) dried thyme
- 1 tsp (2 g) chile flakes
- 1 tsp (2 g) sea salt
- 1 tsp (2 g) black pepper
- ½ cup (45 g) vegan Parmesan cheese or nutritional yeast
- ¼ cup (50 ml) olive oil
- ¼ cup (50 ml) vegan butter, melted

DIPPING SAUCE
- 1 cup (225 g) vegan mayo
- 2 Tbsp (30 ml) ketchup
- ½ tsp (1 g) smoked paprika
- 1 tsp (5 ml) whiskey or apple cider vinegar
- Zest and juice of half a lemon
- ¼ cup (41 g) chives, chopped
- Salt and pepper to taste

GARNISH
- ¼ cup (15 g) parsley, chopped

MAGICAL METHOD

1. Preheat deep fryer to 300 degrees F (150 degrees C). (Alternatively, you can bake. Preheat oven to 340 degrees F [170 degrees C]. Line a baking sheet with parchment paper and set aside.)

2. Skewer each potato. Next, place a knife at one end of each potato, then slice down carefully but not all the way to the skewer (½ inch/1 cm from the skewer). Cut around the potato to create a spiral (or use a potato spiralizer). Gently pull the spiralized potato into a tornado shape.

3. In a small bowl, mix all seasoning ingredients until combined.

4. Fry the potato spirals in the deep fryer for 5 minutes. They should be cooked in the middle but not golden brown.

5. Set the deep fryer to 385 degrees F (180 degrees C). Fry the potatoes for 5 to 6 minutes. Remove from fryer and brush with the seasoning mixture. (If baking, brush the seasoning mixture onto the potatoes, place on the baking sheet and bake for 45 to 50 minutes, turning the skewers every 15 minutes.)

6. Meanwhile, in a small bowl, mix the dipping sauce ingredients until combined. Adjust to taste. Garnish with chopped parsley and enjoy right away.

....

The Kitchen Witch is humming…
"The Goblet of Fire" —Patrick Doyle
....

Fang's Boarhound Treats

First mentioned in *Sorcerer's Stone,* Hagrid's boarhound companion Fang never holds back about showing his affections to visitors, and his gentle demeanor certainly warrants a treat or two. Serve these dog-friendly apple and peanut butter delights to your own furry friend(s), no matter how many heads they have.

NOTE This is a recipe for dogs but can be eaten by drooling humans as well.
PREP TIME overnight YIELD 8 boarhound treats

INGREDIENTS

- ½ cup (125 ml) unsweetened apple sauce
- ½ cup (125 ml) vegan yogurt
- ¼ cup (31 g) apple, finely grated
- ¼ cup (60 g) peanut butter
- 1 Tbsp (15 ml) coconut oil, melted

MAGICAL METHOD

1. In a blender or food processor, add all ingredients and blend until smooth. Transfer the mixture into paw print silicone molds (or another dog-themed mold), filling to the top.

2. Freeze for 4 hours or overnight. Best served on a hot day as a refreshing treat.

The Kitchen Witch is humming…
"Fluffy's Harp" —John Williams

From the Kitchen Witch

You can swap out the grated apple for another dog-friendly fruit like strawberries, blueberries, bananas, raspberries, pears, (water)melon or mango.

MEMORY VIAL

My 9-year-old English Bulldog, Ivy, is such an important part of my life and my work in the kitchen. She is always by my side, waiting on her cute bum, hoping that a piece of food will magically find its way into her Buckbeak. She goes absolutely nuts for cucumber, peanut butter and yogurt. Our bond is unbreakable and I am truly honored to be the mom of this loyal, playful, determined and funny girl.

Stuffed Shrivelfig
Leaves, pg. 80

Greenhouse Salads

Grab your gloves and your pruning shears. For today's Herbology lesson, you'll be conjuring up leafy dishes that just might knock the earmuffs off your professor. As someone seeking out enchanting plant-based options, you'll be forgiven if your stomach gives a bit of a growl as you look at these incredible (and incredibly filling) dishes.

Stay light and refreshed at the lake with a Gillyweed Salad (gill-sprouting not guaranteed), arm yourself against any potential Petrification with a tangy Mandrake Root Salad and chomp away on some Shaved Chinese Chomping Cabbage Salad (you know, before it decides to chomp you).

So start repotting those mandrakes, but be careful! You can never truly know what's flora and who's fauna in these greenhouses...

Counter-Petrification Dressings

Herbal elixirs are carefully coaxed from a variety of plants known for their healing properties, and these whimsical dressings are no exception. They'll do wonders to liven up your next meal—just be sure to save a little in case there's a basilisk sighting nearby.

PREP TIME 5 minutes **COOK TIME** 15 minutes **YIELD** Enough for 3 bottles (1½ cups [360 ml])

MANDRAKE RESTORATIVE DRAUGHT DRESSING

INGREDIENTS

- 1 avocado, halved
- 1 spring onion
- Zest and juice of 1 lime
- ¼ cup (15 g) fresh parsley
- ¼ cup (15 g) fresh mint
- ¼ cup (15 g) fresh coriander
- ½ cup (30 g) fresh basil
- 3 cloves of garlic
- 2 tsp (4 g) nutritional yeast
- ¼ cup (50 ml) avocado oil
- ½ cup (120 g) coconut yogurt
- Sea salt and pepper to taste

MAGICAL METHOD

1. Scoop the avocado flesh into a food processor or blender.
2. Cut the ends off of the spring onion. Note: Instead of discarding the root end, fill up a small glass jar with a little water, drop it in and it will grow back in a few days. Finely chop the onion and add to the avocado.
3. Add the lime zest and juice, fresh herbs (with stalks), garlic, nutritional yeast, oil, yogurt, salt and pepper. Blend until smooth and adjust seasoning to taste. Serve immediately or store in a bottle or jar and refrigerate for up to two days.

CREAMY CURSE-REVERSING DRESSING

INGREDIENTS

- ½ cup (120 g) vegan mayo
- ½ cup (125 ml) oat milk
- 3 Tbsp (17 g) vegan Parmesan
- 1 tsp (5 ml) white wine vinegar
- 1 tsp (5 ml) vegan Worcestershire sauce
- 1 shallot, finely diced
- 2 Tbsp (20 g) capers, finely diced
- Zest and juice of 1 lemon
- 2 cloves of garlic, crushed
- ¼ cup (15 g) fresh dill, chopped
- 1 tsp (2 g) onion powder
- 2 Tbsp (20 g) hemp seeds
- 1 Tbsp (20 g) maple syrup
- Sea salt and white pepper to taste

MAGICAL METHOD

NOTE You can make this dressing by adding all the ingredients to a blender and blending until smooth or by chopping the ingredients roughly.

1. In a small mixing bowl, add the vegan mayo, oat milk, Parmesan, vinegar and Worcestershire sauce. Mix until combined.
2. Mix in the remaining ingredients until combined.

SPICY MANGO RESTORATIVE DRAUGHT DRESSING

INGREDIENTS

- 1 cup (200 g) fresh mango, cubed
- 2 cloves of garlic
- 1 tsp (2 g) freshly grated ginger
- ½ cup (16 g) fresh coriander
- 1 tsp (2 g) chile flakes or cayenne pepper
- ¼ tsp (0.5 g) gojuchang
- Zest and juice of 1 lime
- Zest and juice of 1 orange
- ¼ cup and 3 Tbsp (100 ml) fresh mango juice

1 tsp (2 g) dried mint

1 tsp (2 g) dried mango powder

½ cup (16 g) Thai basil

1 tsp (2 g) sumac

1 tsp (5 ml) ginger syrup (from stem ginger)

1 tsp (5 ml) orange blossom water

Sea salt and pepper to taste

MAGICAL METHOD

In a food processor or blender, add all ingredients and blend until combined. Adjust to taste.

SALAD & DRESSING PAIRING INSPIRATION:

MANDRAKE RESTORATIVE DRAUGHT DRESSING

Buddha bowl, spring salad and broccoli salad

CREAMY CURSE-REVERSING DRESSING

Caesar salad, Cobb salad and pasta salad

SPICY MANGO RESTORATIVE DRAUGHT DRESSING

Noodle salad, tofu lettuce cups and rice salad

The Kitchen Witch is humming...

"The Chamber of Secrets"
—*John Williams*

Mandrake Root Salad

Mandrake, or Mandragora, holds powerful restorative properties for those who have been Petrified or cursed and returns them to their original state. It's also delicious. Layered with tangy, deep pink onions and kale and bursting (literally) with pomegranate seeds, this salad's sure to bring your palate to life.

PREP TIME 10 minutes, 1 day beforehand **COOK TIME** 45 minutes **YIELD** Enough for 4 Herbology students
HERBOLOGY NOTE Neglecting earmuffs is not advised: Put them on right away.

INGREDIENTS

PICKLED RED ONIONS

- 2 red onions
- ½ red chile
- 1 piece of ginger
- 2 cloves of garlic, crushed
- 2 cardamom pods
- 2 star anise
- 4 peppercorns
- 1 bay leaf
- 1 cinnamon stick
- 1 cup (250 ml) apple cider vinegar
- 4 juniper berries
- 1 cup (200 g) granulated sugar
- 1 tsp (2 g) sea salt

SALAD

- 5 cups (1 kg) Jerusalem artichokes, peeled
- 2 Tbsp (30 ml) plus 1 Tbsp (15 ml) olive oil, divided
- 1 tsp (2 g) sea salt
- 1 tsp (2 g) white pepper
- 1 cup (130 g) hazelnuts
- 1 head of Tuscan kale, destemmed and chopped

into stamp-sized pieces
Juice of 1 lemon
- 1 grapefruit, peeled and sliced into wedges
Zest and juice of 1 orange
- 1¾ cups (52.5 g) purple spinach
- 1 cup (250 g) pomegranate seeds
- 1 cup (90 g) vegan Parmesan, shaved

POMEGRANATE DRESSING

Juice of 1 pomegranate
- ½ cup (230 g) pomegranate molasses
- 2 Tbsp (30 ml) balsamic or raspberry vinegar
- 1 Tbsp (10 g) fresh raspberries
- 1 cup (250 ml) walnut oil
Zest and juice of 1 lemon
Salt and pepper to taste
- 2 Tbsp (43 g) maple syrup

GARNISH

Fresh raspberries
Cress

MAGICAL METHOD

NOTE Make the pickled onions the day before for maximum deep color and flavor.

1. Slice the red onions into half-moons.

2. Grab a little bit of olive oil and rub it on your fingertips (to prevent your hands from burning). Slice the chile down the middle, deseed and slice into thin strips.

3. Thinly slice three pieces of ginger. (If organic, no need to peel it.)

From the Kitchen Witch

When handling a large pomegranate, slice in half and hold one half with the cut side down in the palm of your hand. Bash the back of the fruit with your other hand or a wooden spoon. The seeds will fly out. Discard the bitter pith.

4. In a small saucepan on medium-high heat, add garlic, chile, ginger and remaining pickled onion ingredients except for onions and stir until the sugar is dissolved, about 3 to 4 minutes. Simmer and let the flavors infuse for 5 minutes.

5. Fill a jar with the onions, then pour in the hot brine and stir, mixing well. Seal with the lid, then place the jar upside down on the counter for 5 minutes. Let cool completely before placing in the refrigerator.

THE NEXT DAY

6. Preheat oven to 390 degrees F (200 degrees C). Line a baking sheet with a silicone mat or parchment paper.

7. Cut the artichokes into 1-inch (3-cm) cubes. Place the cubes onto the baking sheet. Drizzle with 2 Tbsp olive oil and season with sea salt and white pepper. Roast for 35 minutes until golden brown. During the last 10 minutes of roasting, add the hazelnuts. Let cool completely.

8. In a large mixing bowl, add the kale, lemon juice and 1 Tbsp olive oil. Using your hands, mix until fully combined and set aside.

9. In a griddle pan on high heat, grill grapefruit wedges on both sides until grill lines form, about 3 to 5 minutes on a preheated grill. Remove to a bowl. Add

orange juice and zest, mixing until combined.

10. In a blender or food processor, add the dressing ingredients and blend until smooth. Adjust to taste.

11. In a large serving bowl, add the pickled red onions, kale, roasted mandrake roots (aka artichokes), hazelnuts, grapefruit, spinach, pomegranate seeds and

Parmesan. Toss with dressing and garnish with raspberries and cress before serving.

....

The Kitchen Witch is humming...
"Cornish Pixies" —John Williams
....

Stuffed Shrivelfig Leaves

First mentioned in *Chamber of Secrets*, the Shrivelfig is a purple fruit with blossoms inside that, when skinned, produces a purple liquid useful in potions. Fallen leaves from the Shrivelfig tree also possess remarkable medicinal properties. These plump, fresh figs are served with a zesty and tangy lemon rice immersed in a creamy mint yogurt sauce, making for a light but nonetheless potent pairing.

PREP TIME 45 minutes **COOK TIME** 1 hour and 45 minutes **YIELD** 45 stuffed shrivelfig leaves, enough for 6–8 Herbology students **HERBOLOGY NOTE** Shrivelfigs survive through even the coldest of winters. If you are feeling a little off this winter, let this recipe be a reminder that small sparks of joy can be found in the meals we create for ourselves and loved ones. To indulge in a moment of comfort always lifts the spirit and senses.

INGREDIENTS

- 2 packets vine leaves
- ½ cup (125 ml) plus 2 Tbsp (30 ml) extra-virgin olive oil
- 2 small onions, finely diced
- 1 white onion, finely diced
- ½ fennel stalk, finely diced
- 1 cup and 1 Tbsp (212 g) arborio rice
- Zest and juice of 2 lemons
- 7 cloves of garlic, crushed
- 2 sprigs fresh tarragon
- 3 sprigs thyme
- 2 sprigs oregano
- ½ tsp (1 g) fennel seeds
- 2 cups and 1 Tbsp (515 ml) vegetable stock
- 1 cup (30 g) fresh coriander stalks, chopped
- 3 cups (90 g) baby spinach
- 1 tsp (2 g) sumac
- ½ tsp (0.5 g) dried mint
- 1 cup (30 g) fresh mint, chopped

- ½ cup (15 g) fresh dill, chopped
- 2 Tbsp (28 g) vegan blue cheese or feta (For vegan feta recipe, see Cunning Green Crudité Board on pg. 54.)
- 1 cup (150 g) dried figs, chopped
- 2 tsp (4 g) pomegranate molasses
- ½ cup (15 g) fresh parsley
- Sea salt and pepper to taste
- 1 lemon, sliced
- Juice of 1 lemon

MINT-YOGURT SAUCE

- 2 cups (500 ml) coconut yogurt
- Zest and juice of 1 lime
- 4 cloves of garlic
- 1 tsp (5 ml) agave syrup
- ½ cucumber
- 1 tsp (2 g) ground cumin
- 1 tsp (2 g) dried oregano
- 1 tsp (2 g) dried mint

- 1 Tbsp (15 ml) cold water
- 1 tsp (5 ml) extra-virgin olive oil
- Salt and pepper to taste

GARNISH

- Fresh and dried fig slices
- 2 lemons, cut into wedges
- Fresh dill and parsley, chopped

MAGICAL METHOD

1. Soak the vine leaves in a bowl of lukewarm water for 15 minutes.

2. Meanwhile, in a large frying pan on medium-high heat, add the olive oil and fry the onions until translucent. Add a pinch of salt and pepper, then add the fennel along with another pinch of salt and pepper. Cook on medium-low heat for about 10 minutes, stirring occasionally until caramelized.

3. Add the rice and mix until combined. Turn up the heat to

dill. Crumble in the feta or blue cheese and mix until combined. Stir in the chopped dried figs, molasses and parsley. Finish with an extra squeeze of lemon and sea salt and pepper to taste. Let cool completely on a cold plate.

8. Meanwhile, add the yogurt sauce ingredients to a blender or food processor and blend until smooth. Adjust seasoning to taste. Place in the fridge until ready to serve.

9. To assemble the stuffed vine leaves, place each leaf rough side up. Add 1 Tbsp of filling in the middle and roll the leaf once to cover the filling. Fold in the sides and roll tightly. Place 4 to 5 lemon slices in a large saucepan. Cover with 20 to 25 stuffed leaves. Then, add 5 to 6 more lemon slices, followed by ½ cup (125 ml) olive oil and the juice of 1 lemon. Follow with the second layer of stuffed leaves.

10. Place a plate in the pan to cover the second layer of stuffed leaves, then cover leaves completely with water. Make sure to leave some room in the pan so it doesn't boil over. Cook on medium heat for 45 to 50 minutes. If you see the water has evaporated, add a bit more.

11. Serve hot or cold with the refreshing yogurt sauce.

⋯⋯⋯⋯⋯⋯⋯⋯⋯⋯⋯⋯⋯⋯⋯⋯⋯

The Kitchen Witch is humming…
"Reunion of Friends" —*John Williams*

⋯⋯⋯⋯⋯⋯⋯⋯⋯⋯⋯⋯⋯⋯⋯⋯⋯

medium-high and toast the rice for 3 minutes. Deglaze the pan with lemon juice. Add the garlic and mix until combined.

4. Rip or shred the leaves from the tarragon, thyme and oregano and add to the pan. Add the fennel seeds, then mix until fragrant. The kitchen will smell amazing.

5. In another saucepan on medium-high heat, add the vegetable stock and let simmer for 10 to 15 minutes.

6. Meanwhile, add the coriander to the pan with the rice, then add a pinch of salt and pepper. Add a ladle of stock at a time to the rice and stir vigorously with a wooden spoon. Add another ladle of stock once the previous one has evaporated. Repeat this cycle for 10 minutes. (Remember to undercook the rice because the vine leaves will be steamed.)

7. Add the spinach to the rice (the residual heat will wilt the leaves). Sprinkle in the sumac, dried mint, lemon zest, fresh mint and

Caramelized Devil's Snare

First encountered in *Sorcerer's Stone*, this bewitched plant covered in dark,
writhing tendrils bent on ensnaring you is not easily forgotten. Should you encounter one,
keep calm and snip off a few vines to prepare this devilishly delicious salad.

PREP TIME 15 minutes **COOK TIME** 45 minutes **YIELD** Enough for 3–4 Herbology students

INGREDIENTS

7½ cups (1 kg) salsify
1 lemon
2 Tbsp (30 ml) extra-virgin olive oil
2 cups (150 g) chanterelle mushrooms
Salt and pepper to taste
4 sprigs fresh thyme
2 tsp (10 ml) dark soy sauce
1 tsp (5 ml) cooking sake
1 cup (200 g) beluga lentils, rinsed
2 bay leaves
2 tsp (4 g) ras el hanout
2 Tbsp (20 g) chopped chives
1 Tbsp (14 g) vegan butter
½ tsp (1 g) freshly grated nutmeg
2 tsp (4 g) cumin seeds
2 tsp (10 g) maple syrup
1 Braeburn apple
1 Granny Smith apple
1 cup (150 g) walnuts
½ cup (16 g) fresh parsley, finely chopped
1 cup (150 g) medjool dates, destoned and cut into strips

BLACK GARLIC DRESSING

1 bulb of smoked black garlic
2 tsp (4 g) Dijon mustard
½ cup (125 ml) fresh apple juice
2 tsp (10 ml) red wine vinegar
1 cup (250 ml) walnut oil
1 tsp (2 g) smoked sea salt
1 tsp (2 g) black pepper
Zest and juice of 1 lemon
1 tsp (2 g) nigella seeds

GARNISH

Microgreens or cress
Extra-virgin olive oil

MAGICAL METHOD

1. Peel the rough skin off the salsify, cut off woody ends and cut each in half or thirds. Fill a large storage container with cold water.
2. Cut the lemon in half and squeeze out all the juice. Drop the halves into the container and add the peeled salsify. This will prevent it from getting brown while you prepare the other ingredients.
3. Cut the mushrooms in half from top to bottom (keep the small ones whole). Cut off the woody ends and brush off excess dirt. (Note: Never wash your mushrooms or they will become soggy.)
4. In a large frying pan on medium heat, add 1 Tbsp of olive oil followed by the mushrooms. Add a pinch of salt and pepper and fry for 7 minutes, turning every 2 minutes. Season with 1 sprig of thyme, dark soy sauce and sake and let cook 2 to 3 minutes. Remove from heat, season to taste and let mushrooms cool down completely. Set aside.
5. Fill a large saucepan with water on medium-high heat. Add salt

and bring to a boil. Add beluga lentils and bay leaves, then turn heat to medium and cook for 20 minutes. Remove from heat and let cool to room temperature. Season with olive oil, salt and pepper, ras el hanout and chopped chives. Set aside until serving.

6. Wash the large frying pan and dry off the salsify. On medium-high heat, add 1 Tbsp of olive oil and 1 Tbsp vegan butter to the large frying pan. Fry the salsify, turning every few minutes, for 10 minutes or until all sides are browned. Season with freshly grated nutmeg and cumin seeds, then mix until coated. Add remaining thyme and mix until combined.

7. Turn heat to medium-low and add maple syrup, stirring until coated. Cook for 10 minutes or until caramelized. Season with salt and pepper.

8. Meanwhile, core and thinly slice the apples. Add a few drops of lemon juice so that they do not brown and set aside.

9. Add the lentils, walnuts and parsley to the caramelized salsify in the pan, mix until combined and turn off the heat.

10. In a medium-large mixing bowl, add the black garlic and mustard. Mix until combined into a paste. Pour in the apple juice, red wine vinegar and walnut oil. Mix until combined. Season with the smoked sea salt, black pepper and lemon zest and juice.

Mix again. Add the nigella seeds. (Note: Toast the seeds for 1 or 2 minutes in a dry frying pan until they pop for extra flavor.)

11. Arrange the salsify, lentils and walnuts on a large serving platter. Drizzle with dressing, then place the mushrooms on top. Sprinkle with dates. Artfully arrange the apple slices around and in between the salsify. Garnish with microgreens or cress, finish with a dash of extra virgin olive oil and serve immediately.

·······························

The Kitchen Witch is humming…
"In the Devil's Snare and the Flying Keys" —John Williams

·······························

Shaved Chinese Chomping Cabbage Salad

It's harvest time in Greenhouse 5. The teething Chinese Chomping Cabbages, as mentioned in *Order of the Phoenix*, are munching bits of the carrot tops— clearly, it's a plant-eat-plant world, and you'd better get moving before these greens notice what you're up to. Handle this salad with peanut dressing with care because not everyone will want to share!

PREP TIME 10 minutes   **COOK TIME** 35 minutes   **YIELD** Enough for 2 hungry witches or wizards

INGREDIENTS

CRISPY POTATOES

- 2 Tbsp (30 ml) sesame oil
- 2 tsp (4 g) garlic powder
- 1 tsp (2 g) smoked paprika
- 1 tsp (2 g) Chinese five spice
- Salt and pepper to taste
- 5 cups (1 kg) waxed and unpeeled potatoes, cut into 0.7-inch (2-cm) cubes
- 1 cup (150 g) cashews
- ½ cup (75 g) peanuts

SALAD

- 2 cups (200 g) bean sprouts
- 1 cup (200 g) green beans
- 1 cucumber
- 1 Chinese cabbage
- ⅔ cup (150 g) smoked tempeh, cut into 0.7-inch (2-cm) cubes
- 2 tsp (4 g) Chinese five spice
- 2 tsp (4 g) garlic powder
- 1 tsp (2 g) smoked paprika
- 1 tsp (2 g) dried laos
- 1 tsp (2 g) dried ginger
- 1 tsp (2 g) chile flakes

- 1 cup (250 g) medium-firm tofu, pressed and cut into 0.7-inch (2-cm) cubes
- 2 Tbsp (30 ml) dark soy sauce
- 1 Tbsp (15 ml) plum sauce
- 1 medium carrot, peeled into ribbons
- 1 mango, peeled, diced into 0.3-inch (1-cm) cubes
- 3 cups (100 g) fresh coriander
- 3 cups (100 g) fresh Thai basil
- 2 cups (65 g) fresh mint

PEANUT DRESSING

- 1½ cups (360 g) smooth peanut butter
- Zest and juice of 2 limes
- 1 Tbsp (15 ml) light soy sauce
- 1 Tbsp (10 g) mirin
- 1 tsp (2 g) chile flakes
- 1 tsp (2 g) vegan sambal badjak
- 2 tsp (6 ml) agave syrup
- 1 cup (250 ml) coconut water
- 2 tsp (10 ml) sesame oil
- 2 tsp (10 ml) rice wine vinegar
- 4 cloves of garlic
- 2 tsp (4 g) freshly grated ginger

- 2 tsp (4 g) Chinese five spice

GARNISH

- 2 cups (340 g) cassava chips, crushed
- 1 lime, cut into wedges
- 2 Tbsp (20 g) white sesame seeds

MAGICAL METHOD

1. Preheat oven to 425 degrees F (220 degrees C). Line a baking sheet with a silicone mat or parchment paper. Place the potatoes on the baking sheet. Add a shot of olive oil followed by the potato spices, salt and pepper, and mix well with your hands. Roast for 25 minutes or until crispy and golden brown; for the last 5 minutes, add the cashews and peanuts. Let cool completely.

2. In a small mixing bowl, add the bean sprouts. Pour 3 cups (750 ml) boiling water onto the sprouts and let steep for 10 minutes. Drain, squeeze out the moisture and set aside.

3. Fill up a large saucepan with water on medium-high heat and let it come to a boil. Blanch the green beans for roughly 5 to 6 minutes. Put in a sieve, rinse with cold water and set aside.

4. Smash your cucumber: First, slice in half lengthwise and remove the seeds with a knife or spoon. Put the cucumber cut side down and smash slightly with the knife. Cut the smashed cucumber diagonally and set aside.

5. Fill a large saucepan with water halfway and boil on medium-high heat. When the water boils, place a bamboo steamer on top.

6. Tear off the outer leaves of the cabbage and stack in the bamboo steamer. Steam for 10 minutes on medium-high. Add the tempeh and cook for 5 minutes. Remove from heat, place on a large platter and let cool.

7. Finely slice the rest of the cabbage into strips (as thin as possible) and set aside.

8. Sprinkle the Chinese five spice, garlic powder, smoked paprika, laos, ginger and chile flakes over the tofu. Add the cooled tempeh pieces. Mix until combined.

9. In a large frying pan with sesame or avocado oil on medium heat, add the tofu and tempeh and fry for about 12 minutes, stirring occasionally, until golden brown. Add the soy sauce and plum sauce and cook, stirring, for 3 minutes.

Remove from heat and set aside.

10. In a blender or food processor, add the dressing ingredients and blend until smooth. Note: Slightly heating up the peanut butter helps it blend more easily. Adjust to taste.

11. Arrange the steamed cabbage leaves on a large serving platter. Feel free to cut the steamed leaves into four smaller pieces for easier eating. Add the thinly sliced cabbage, bean sprouts, cucumber, carrot, mango, crispy potatoes, tofu, tempeh, fresh herbs and roasted nuts, then mix until combined.

12. Drizzle liberally with peanut dressing and garnish with crushed cassava chips, lime wedges and sesame seeds. Serve and enjoy immediately.

....

The Kitchen Witch is humming...
"Leaving Hogwarts" —John Williams
....

Gillyweed Salad

Gathering greens that grow beneath the surface of the Mediterranean Sea is sure to prepare you for an aquatic adventure that could rival Harry's in *Goblet of Fire*. The saltiness of the gillyweed (well, hijiki and wakame) and the sea vegetable textures, all drenched in a mouthwatering dressing, will make you want to dive right in.

PREP TIME 20 minutes   **COOK TIME** 45 minutes   **YIELD** Enough for 2 Triwizard champions

INGREDIENTS

- 4 cups (100 g) wakame
- 2 cups (50 g) hijiki
- 4 cups (100 g) samphire
- 1 lime, halved
- 2 spring onions, sliced
- 3 cups (125 g) green tea or seaweed noodles
- 2 tsp (30 ml) roasted sesame oil
- 2 cups (50 g) fresh coriander
- 1 cucumber
- 1 zucchini, spiralized

SESAME DRESSING

- ½ cup (120 g) white sesame tahini
- Zest and juice of 2 limes
- 1 cup (240 g) vegan mayo
- ½ cup (125 ml) lukewarm water
- 4 cloves of garlic
- 2 Tbsp (30 ml) roasted sesame oil
- 1 tsp (2 g) freshly grated ginger
- 2 tsp (10 ml) rice wine vinegar
- 1 Tbsp (10 g) mirin

- 1 tsp (2 g) sea salt or soy sauce
- 1 tsp (2 g) chili paste
- ½ cup (25 g) fresh coriander, chopped
- 2 Tbsp (20 g) roasted white sesame seeds

GARNISH

- 4 Japanese limes
- 2 Tbsp (20 g) furikake
- Sesame seeds
- 1 cup (100 g) crispy green nori crinkles
- ½ cup (50 g) nori rice crisps, crushed

MAGICAL METHOD

1. Place the wakame in a large mixing bowl. Cover with boiling water and let soak for at least 15 minutes.

2. Fill a small saucepan with water and bring to a boil on medium-high heat. Once it reaches a boil, bring the heat down to low, add the hijiki and cook for 15 minutes.

Let cool completely before adding to the salad.

3. In a small frying pan on medium-high heat, add olive oil, then add the samphire and cook for 3 to 4 minutes. Add freshly cracked pepper to taste, the juice of half a lime and one spring onion. Set aside and let cool completely.

4. Fill a medium-sized saucepan with water and bring to a boil on medium-high heat. Add the noodles and cook according to the packet instructions, stirring occasionally so the noodles don't stick together. Drain, then rinse under cold water. Add 1 tsp sesame oil to the noodles and mix.

5. Squeeze the excess water out of the wakame and rinse under cold water.

6. Add the coriander to the soaked wakame in a small mixing bowl. Add 1 tsp sesame oil, the second spring onion and cracked black pepper. Mix until combined. Add the juice of half a lime and adjust to taste.

7. Slice the cucumber in half lengthwise, scooping out the seeds with a small spoon, and chop into half-moons.

8. Place the vegetables on a large serving platter. Set aside or refrigerate until needed.

9. Add all dressing ingredients except the roasted sesame seeds to a blender or food processor and blend until smooth and creamy. Add the sesame seeds and mix until combined. Adjust to taste.

10. Pour the sesame dressing over the vegetable platter or serve it on the side. Garnish with limes, furikake, sesame seeds, and nori rice crinkles and crisps. Best enjoyed immediately.

....

The Kitchen Witch is humming...
"The Black Lake" — Patrick Doyle

....

From the Kitchen Witch

Seaweed has many benefits to our overall well-being. While preparing this Gillyweed salad, take a moment to honor the endless bounty of the sea by considering all the plants and creatures that lurk in its depths.

Start-of-Term Feast,
pg. 90

Main Feasts

A fter a particularly tiring day of Charms and Divination, you're eager to dive into the spellbinding feasts the school of witchcraft and wizardry is famous for. But what if this school of magic doesn't offer plant-based options? Fortunately, these main feasts inspired by the world of *Harry Potter* will ensure you are satisfied as you dreamily wander back to your common room!

Tuck in with your new northern friends from Durmstrang with a Heartwarming Goulash, be the subject of envy from the ghosts as you dive into the full Start-of-Term Feast and enjoy a plant-based twist on a British classic with a warm and fluffy Shepherd's Pie.

Listen up to the start-of-term notices, avoid the third-floor corridor on the right-hand side and let the feast begin!

Start-of-Term Feast

Each September 1, as students are ushered into the Great Hall (as Harry is in *Sorcerer's Stone*), they are enraptured by the space, with its four long tables and vast enchanted ceiling that seems to cheat time and space. Once they've finished eating a full English roast with all the trimmings, they're part of the Hogwarts family—even those who don't eat roast.

PREP TIME 30 minutes **COOK TIME** 3 hours to overnight **YIELD** Enough for 4–6 witches and wizards

ENGLISH ROAST
INGREDIENTS
- 2 medium shallots, peeled and quartered
- 7 cloves of garlic
- 4 cups (950 ml) mushroom broth
- ¼ cup plus 3 Tbsp (100 ml) dark soy sauce
- 1 cup (250 ml) vegan red wine
- ¼ cup (50 ml) beetroot juice
- Zest of 1 clementine
- 2 bay leaves
- 2 star anise
- 5 black peppercorns
- 5 juniper berries
- 2 sprigs thyme
- 2 sprigs rosemary
- 1 tsp (2 g) Marmite
- 1 Tbsp (15 ml) mushroom chili oil
- 2 Tbsp (30 ml) olive oil
- Salt and pepper to taste
- 6 cups (156 g) dehydrated lion's mane mushrooms

GARNISH
- Microgreens
- Cress
- Chopped parsley
- Sauerkraut
- Chopped chives

MAGICAL METHOD
1. In a large saucepan on medium-high heat, combine all ingredients expect for lion's mane mushrooms, salt and pepper. Stir until combined. Season with salt and pepper. Bring to a boil, then set heat to low. Simmer for about 20 minutes.

2. Meanwhile, slice the lion's mane mushrooms about as thin as a coin, cutting against the grain. After the mixture in the saucepan has simmered for 20 minutes, add the mushrooms and mix well. Cover with lid and simmer for 30 minutes.

3. Transfer the mushrooms to a cutting board (ideally one with grooves for catching liquid) and cover with parchment paper. Using heavy books or a cast iron pan, press the juices out of the mushrooms for at least 1 hour (preferably overnight).

ROASTED VEGETABLES
INGREDIENTS
- 2 bell peppers, cut into thick strips
- 1 small pumpkin, peeled, deseeded and diced into 1.1-inch (3-cm) cubes
- 1 red onion, quartered
- 1 yellow zucchini
- 1 green zucchini
- 2 parsnips, peeled and quartered
- 3 cups (264 g) Brussels sprouts, ends chopped, outer leaves removed
- Salt and pepper to taste
- ½ cup (120 ml) olive oil
- 1 Tbsp (20 g) maple syrup
- 1 sprig fresh rosemary
- 4 fresh sage leaves
- 2 sprigs fresh thyme

MAGICAL METHOD

1. Preheat oven to 390 degrees F (200 degrees C).

2. Line a baking sheet with parchment paper. Place the vegetables on the baking sheet and season with salt and pepper. Drizzle with olive oil and maple syrup, then mix to coat. Roast for 30 minutes.

3. Shake the baking sheet to turn the vegetables, then add rosemary, sage and thyme. Roast for 15 minutes.

ROASTED POTATOES

INGREDIENTS

  5 cups (1 kg) Maris Piper potatoes, peeled
     Salt and pepper to taste

  1 cup (250 ml) olive oil

  1 bulb of garlic

  2 sprigs rosemary
     Zest of 1 clementine

MAGICAL METHOD

1. Fill a large saucepan with water and add a pinch of salt. Set heat to medium-high and let come to a boil. Add the potatoes and cook for 10 minutes. Drain, then shake the pan to roughen up the edges (or skin, if leaving whole).

2. Preheat oven to 430 degrees F (220 degrees C).

3. Line a baking sheet with parchment paper and spread out the potatoes in a single layer. Season with salt, pepper and olive oil. Add the garlic. Roast for 30 minutes. Remove from oven. Using a potato masher, slightly press down on the potatoes. Add rosemary and clementine zest. Roast for another 15 minutes.

YORKSHIRE PUDDING

INGREDIENTS

  ½ cup plus 1½ Tbsp (75 g) corn flour

  ½ cup plus 1½ Tbsp (75 g) self-raising flour

  2 tsp (4 g) baking powder

  ½ tsp (1 g) curry powder
     Salt and pepper to taste

  ⅔ cup plus 3 Tbsp (200 ml) almond milk

  12 Tbsp (180 ml) canola oil

MAGICAL METHOD

In a large mixing bowl, combine the dry ingredients, then whisk in the milk until it takes on the consistency of pancake batter, about 1 to 1½ minutes. Season with salt and pepper and refrigerate until needed. When you're ready to bake, transfer the batter into a pouring pitcher or jug for easy pouring.

GRAVY

INGREDIENTS

  1 Tbsp (15 ml) olive oil

  2 Tbsp (28 g) vegan butter

  2 medium carrots, quartered

  3 shallots, quartered

  3¼ cups (250 g) chestnut mushrooms, quartered

  1 leek, quartered

  6 cloves of garlic, crushed
     Salt and pepper to taste

  ¼ cup (30 g) plain flour

  2 Tbsp (32 g) tomato paste

  ½ cup (125 ml) vegan red wine

  2 cups, plus 1 Tbsp (515 ml) vegetable stock

  1 tsp (2 g) Marmite

  2 bay leaves

  1 sprig rosemary

  2 sprigs fresh thyme

  2 fresh sage leaves

  ¼ cup (19 g) dried porcini mushrooms, quartered

  ½ tsp (1 g) freshly grated nutmeg
     Peel and juice of 1 clementine

MAGICAL METHOD

1. In a large saucepan with olive oil on medium-high heat, melt the vegan butter, about 1 minute. Add the carrots, shallots, chestnut mushrooms, leek and garlic. Season with salt and pepper and cook for 15 minutes to caramelize, stirring occasionally.

2. Add the flour and cook for 5 minutes, stirring often. Add the tomato paste and cook for 3 minutes.

3. Deglaze the pan with red wine,

TO FINISH THE FEAST...

1. Preheat oven to 430 degrees F (220 degrees C).

2. Spoon 1 tsp of canola oil into each well of a muffin tin. Place in the oven and let preheat for 10 minutes.

3. Remove the muffin tin. Working quickly, fill each well one-third of the way up with Yorkshire pudding batter, then place the tin back into the oven. Set oven to 375 degrees F (190 degrees C) and bake for 16 minutes. Serve immediately after baking.

4. Meanwhile, remove the weight from the mushroom slices.

5. In a large frying pan with olive oil on medium-high heat, add vegan butter and pressed mushroom slices to the pan, taking care not to overcrowd. Season on both sides with salt and pepper, then fry each side for 2 to 3 minutes. Serve immediately with Yorkshire pudding.

6. Arrange all the wonderful feast elements on a large platter, add garnishes and serve.

....

The Kitchen Witch is humming...
"Entry into the Great Hall and the Banquet" —*John Williams*
....

being sure to scrape up all the flavor from the bottom of the pan. When most of the liquid has evaporated, stir in the stock, Marmite, bay leaves, fresh herbs, dried porcini mushrooms, nutmeg, clementine peel and juice, salt and pepper. Set heat to low and cook

for 30 minutes.

4. Pour the gravy through a sieve. Use a spoon to press the vegetables and extract extra flavor. Return the gravy to the stove on low heat until serving.

The Great Feast

The cozy, welcoming atmosphere of the Three Broomsticks on a winter day is wonderfully described in *Prisoner of Azkaban*. As students warm themselves with butterbeer, Madam Rosmerta weaves through the crowd hefting platters of drinks and pub grub just like this classic feast.

PREP TIME 15 minutes **COOK TIME** 1 hour 30 minutes **YIELD** Enough for 6 witches and wizards

BBQ SAUCE

INGREDIENTS

- 1 red onion, finely diced
  Salt and pepper to taste
- 6 cloves of garlic, crushed
- 1 tsp (2 g) smoked paprika
- 1 tsp (2 g) Chinese five spice
- 1 tsp (2 g) onion powder
- 1 tsp (2 g) garlic powder
- 2 Tbsp (30 ml) whiskey
- ¼ cup (50 ml) apple cider vinegar
- 2 cups (470 g) ketchup
- 1 Tbsp (15 ml) vegan Worcestershire sauce
- 2 tsp (4 g) Dijon mustard
- ¼ cup (55 g) brown sugar
- 1 bay leaf
- 1 Tbsp (10 g) apricot jam
- ½ cup (125 ml) dark molasses
  Zest and juice of 1 orange
- 2 drops liquid smoke

MAGICAL METHOD

1. In a medium-sized saucepan with olive oil on medium-high heat, add the red onion and season with salt and pepper. Cook until fragrant and translucent, about 6 to 7 minutes.

2. Stir in the spices. Deglaze the pan with whiskey and apple cider vinegar, then stir in ketchup, Worcestershire sauce, mustard and brown sugar.

3. Set heat to medium-low. Stir in the bay leaf, apricot jam, dark molasses, orange zest and juice and liquid smoke. Season to taste with salt and pepper. Cook for 5 minutes. Once thickened, let cool completely.

SPARE RIBS

INGREDIENTS

- 2¾ cups (600 g) vegan mince
- 2 cans jackfruit in brine
- 2 tsp (10 ml) mushrooms in chili oil
- 1 tsp (2 g) Dijon mustard
- ½ tsp (1 g) white miso paste
- 7 cloves of smoked garlic, crushed
- 1 white onion, finely diced
- 2 tsp (4 g) smoked paprika
- 1 tsp (2 g) tamarind powder
- 1 tsp (2 g) fennel seeds
- 1 tsp (2 g) garlic powder
- 1 tsp (2 g) dried tarragon
- 1 tsp (2 g) freshly grated nutmeg
- 2 tsp (4 g) ground dried mushrooms
- 1 tsp (2 g) chile flakes
- ½ tsp (1 g) cayenne powder
- 1 tsp (2 g) ground coriander
- 1 tsp (2 g) ground cumin
- 1 tsp (2 g) dried marjoram
  Salt and pepper to taste
- 8–10 lemongrass "bones," halved

MAGICAL METHOD

1. Preheat oven to 355 degrees F (180 degrees C). In a large mixing bowl, add the vegan mince. Rinse the jackfruit under cold water and deseed. Tear jackfruit into small pieces and add to the mince along all other ribs ingredients except lemongrass bones. Using your hands, mix until well combined.

2. Transfer mixture to a baking sheet lined with baking paper, then shape into a rectangle about 8.2 inches (21 cm) long and 2.3 inches (6 cm) thick. Poke the lemongrass bones into the sides of the spare rib in a way that resembles the bones of a rack of ribs. Use the palm of your hand to make 2-cm indentations along the top to delineate each rib. Brush the spare ribs with BBQ sauce until well coated, then bake for 40 to 45 minutes until golden brown and caramelized.

3. Cut the spare ribs into four pieces.

CORN ON THE COB
INGREDIENTS

    4   ears of corn
    ½   cup (115 g) vegan butter, room
          temperature
          Zest and juice of 2 limes
    ½   cup (64 g) fresh coriander
          with stalks, finely chopped
    1   tsp (2 g) chile flakes
    ½   tsp (1 g) sea salt
          Salt and pepper to taste
    ¼   tsp (0.5 g) white miso paste
    ½   tsp (1 g) maple syrup
    4   cloves of garlic, crushed

MAGICAL METHOD

1. Boil a large saucepan of water on

medium-high heat, add the corn and cook for 25 minutes. Let cool on a plate.

2. Meanwhile, in a small mixing bowl, combine butter, lime juice and zest, coriander, chile flakes and sea salt. Season to taste with salt and pepper, then stir in miso paste, maple syrup and garlic until well combined. Rub this spiced butter generously across each of the corn cobs.

3. In a griddle pan on medium-high heat, grill the corn on all sides for 2 minutes, then cut the corn cobs in half. Keep warm until serving.

CHICKEN WINGS
INGREDIENTS

    1   tsp (2 g) sweet smoked
          paprika
    ½   tsp (1 g) garlic powder
    ½   tsp (1 g) onion powder
    ½   tsp (1 g) chile flakes
    ½   tsp (1 g) ground cumin
    ½   tsp (1 g) ras el hanout
          Salt and pepper to taste
    4   cups (300 g) oyster
          mushrooms
    1   cup (240 ml) oat milk
    1   Tbsp (15 ml) fresh lemon juice
          Salt and pepper to taste
    1   cup (28 g) plain cornflakes
    1   cup (120 g) plain flour
    ½   tsp (1 g) garlic powder
    ½   tsp (1 g) onion powder
    ¼   tsp (0.5 g) smoked paprika
          Salt and pepper
    4   cups plus 3 Tbsp (1 L)
          canola oil

MAGICAL METHOD

1. In a medium mixing bowl, mix the paprika, garlic and onion powders, chile flakes, cumin, ras el hanout, salt and pepper to taste. Coat the mushrooms in the rub and set aside.

2. In a separate mixing bowl, add oat milk, lemon juice, salt and pepper to taste and whisk until the milk curdles like buttermilk.

3. In a food processor, add the cornflakes, flour, garlic and onion powders, paprika, salt and pepper to taste. Pulse 4 to 5 times, then transfer to a large mixing bowl.

4. Heat the canola oil to 355 degrees F (180 degrees C) in a deep fryer or large heavy pan. Drag each mushroom through the buttermilk, coating well, then coat with the cornflake mixture. You can repeat this step or place directly in the deep fryer.

5. Cook each mushroom for 5 to 6 minutes until golden brown and crispy. Transfer mushrooms to a plate with a kitchen towel; sprinkle with salt.

TO FINISH THE FEAST...
Garnish feast with fresh coriander and serve with extra BBQ sauce.

....

The Kitchen Witch is humming...
"Daytrip to Hogsmeade"
—*The Mudbloods*

....

Bangers & Mash

This beloved English staple, which Harry tucks into at Hogwarts
in *Order of the Phoenix*, is enjoyed by wizards and Muggles alike, whether at home,
school or, ideally, in the comfort of a cozy pub like the Leaky Cauldron. These thick,
artisanal bangers and velvety mash served with the most flavorsome gravy
will make anyone feel right at home.

PREP TIME 20 minutes   **COOK TIME** 1 hour 30 minutes   **YIELD** Enough for 6–8 pub customers

INGREDIENTS

BANGERS

- 1 red onion, finely diced
- 8 cloves of garlic, crushed
- 2 tsp (4 g) sweet smoked paprika
- 1 tsp (2 g) fennel seeds
- ½ tsp (1 g) freshly grated nutmeg
- ½ tsp (1 g) black pepper
- 1 tsp (2 g) dried thyme
- 1 tsp (2 g) sea salt
- 1 tsp (2 g) ground cumin
- 1 tsp (2 g) dried oregano
- 1 tsp (2 g) dried basil
- 1 tsp (2 g) dried marjoram
  Zest of 1 lemon
- 1 cup plus ½ Tbsp (45 g) soy curls
- 2 tsp (4 g) dried porcini mushrooms, chopped
- 1 cup (80 g) rolled oats
- 6 sundried tomatoes
- 2½ Tbsp (25 g) pecans
- 5 Tbsp (45 g) dried cranberry and almond nut mix
- 1 Tbsp (10 g) vegan pesto
- 2 Tbsp (11 g) vegan Parmesan
- 1 tsp (2 g) balsamic glaze

- 5½ cups (1 kg) white beans, cooked
- 1 Tbsp (10 g) psyllium husk

BANGER SKIN

- 8 pieces of rice paper

MASH

- 7½ cups (1.5 kg) floury potatoes, peeled and quartered
- ¼ cup (56 g) vegan butter
- ½ cup (115 ml) oat cream
- ½ cup (45 g) vegan grated Parmesan
- ¼ tsp (0.5 g) freshly grated nutmeg
- 1 Tbsp (10 g) Dijon mustard
  Salt and pepper to taste

GRAVY

- 1 Tbsp (15 ml) olive oil
- 2 red onions, sliced into half-moons
- 1 cup (75 g) dried porcini mushrooms
- 6 cloves of garlic, crushed
- 2 sprigs thyme, finely chopped

- 1 sprig rosemary, finely chopped
- 2 sage leaves, finely chopped
- 1 Tbsp (15 g) tomato paste
- 1 Tbsp (20 g) maple syrup
- 1 Tbsp (10 g) English mustard powder
- 2 bay leaves
- 1 cup (250 ml) stout beer
- 1 Tbsp (10 g) white miso paste
- 1 Tbsp (10 g) Marmite
- 1¼ cups (300 ml) mushroom stock
- 1 tsp (2 g) corn starch
- 1 Tbsp (15 ml) water
- 1 tsp (2 g) freshly grated nutmeg
  Salt and pepper to taste

PEAS

- 4 cups (720 g) frozen peas
- 1 spring onion, sliced
  Zest and juice of 1 lemon
- 4 cloves of garlic, crushed
- 2 sprigs fresh mint, finely chopped
  Salt and pepper to taste

GARNISH

    Chopped parsley

MAGICAL METHOD

1. In a large frying pan with olive oil on medium-high heat, add the onion. Season with salt and pepper. Cook until translucent, about 8 to 10 minutes. Mix in the garlic, dried spices and lemon zest. Add a bit more olive oil, stirring to release the flavor. Cook for 2 to 3 minutes, then remove from heat and let cool completely.

2. Place the dehydrated soy curls and porcini mushrooms in a small mixing bowl, then pour in boiled water. Cover and steep for 10 minutes.

3. In a food processor, blend the rolled oats into fine crumbs (but not so much that it resembles flour—you still want some texture). Transfer to a mixing bowl and set aside.

4. In the same food processor, add the rehydrated soy curls and mushrooms, tomatoes, pecans, cranberry mix, pesto, Parmesan and balsamic glaze.

5. Drain and rinse the white beans and add to the food processor. Blend until smooth. Add the onion mixture, then blend until incorporated. Transfer mixture to the bowl with the oats. Use your hands to combine.

6. Place the psyllium husk in a small bowl and cover with water. Mix until combined and let stand

for 2 to 3 minutes. Add to the sausage mixture.

7. Divide the sausage mixture into eight parts, each weighing 2.9 oz (85 g). Roll each piece into a thick sausage shape, about 4.3 inches (11 cm) long.

8. Fill a large pan or mixing bowl with cold water, then soak the pieces of rice paper one by one for 20 to 25 seconds.

9. Place each sausage portion on a sheet of soaked rice paper. Fold the rice paper tightly over and around the sausage until the sausage is covered.

10. In a large frying pan with olive oil and vegan butter on medium-high heat, add the sausages and cook for 3 minutes on each side or until crispy and golden. Keep warm until serving or refrigerate until needed.

11. Bring a large pan of water to a boil and add the potatoes. Cook until soft for 12 to 15 minutes. Drain the water, then add vegan butter and oat cream. Mash until there are no lumps left, then stir with a wooden spoon until combined. Season with vegan Parmesan, nutmeg, mustard, salt and pepper. Set aside.

12. In a medium-size saucepan with olive oil on medium-high heat, cook the onions for about 10 to 15 minutes or until caramelized. Season with salt and stir occasionally.

13. Add the porcini mushrooms

to a small bowl, then cover with 1 cup (200 ml) of boiling water. Steep for 10 minutes, then remove the mushrooms from the water (save the water!). Finely slice the mushrooms and add to the pan with the onions.

14. Add the garlic and stir until combined. Add the thyme, rosemary and sage and stir until fragrant. Add the tomato paste and cook for 3 minutes. Stir in the maple syrup, mustard powder, bay leaves and beer. Set the heat to medium-low, then stir in the miso paste and Marmite. Cook for 2 minutes. Add the reserved mushroom water and mushroom stock and cook for 5 minutes.

15. In a small bowl, whisk together cornstarch and 1 Tbsp (15 ml) water to form a paste for thickening the gravy. Whisk the paste into the gravy and set heat to low. Season gravy with nutmeg, salt and pepper. Keep warm until serving.

16. In a medium-sized saucepan with olive oil on medium heat, cook the frozen peas for about 5 minutes. Add the onion, lemon juice and zest, garlic and mint. Season with salt and pepper.

17. Serve each portion with a generous dollop of mashed potatoes, one or two sausages topped with gravy and a side of peas. Garnish with parsley and enjoy immediately.

Shepherd's Pie

On pretty much any evening, much like the night Harry arrives at Diagon Alley on the Knight Bus in *Prisoner of Azkaban*, the Leaky Cauldron is a happy haunt for those seeking a pint and a bite. Find a cozy nook to call your own, grab your favorite beer and prepare to dig into this English comfort classic.

PREP TIME 10 minutes   **COOK TIME** 90 minutes   **YIELD** Enough for 6–8 witches and wizards

INGREDIENTS
FILLING

- 1 red onion, sliced into half-moons
-    Salt and pepper to taste
- 3 celery sticks, finely diced
- 2 medium carrots, finely diced
- 8 cloves of smoked garlic, crushed
- 2 tsp (4 g) dried oregano
- 1 tsp (2 g) dried basil
- 1 tsp (2 g) onion powder
- 1 tsp (2 g) garlic powder
- 1 tsp (2 g) dried marjoram
- ½ tsp (1 g) dried mint
- ½ tsp (1 g) dried sage
- 1½ cups (200 g) vegan mince

- 2 sprigs fresh thyme
- ½ tsp (1 g) fresh rosemary, finely chopped (about 1 sprig)
- 2 Tbsp (32 g) tomato paste
- ½ cup (125 ml) vegan red wine
- 2 bay leaves
- 1 star anise
- 1 cinnamon stick
- 2 drops of liquid smoke
- 2 cups (500 ml) mushroom broth
- 1 tsp (5 ml) vegan Worcestershire sauce
- 2 tsp (10 g) maple syrup
- 2 tsp (4 g) instant coffee
- ½ cup (90 g) red lentils
- 1 tsp (2 g) smoked paprika
- ½ tsp (1 g) freshly grated nutmeg

- 1 tsp (2 g) Marmite
-    Zest and juice of 1 orange

MASHED TOPPING

- 5 cups (1 kg) floury potatoes, peeled
- ½ cup (125 ml) oat cream
- 2 Tbsp (20 g) vegan butter
- 1 tsp (2 g) English mustard
- ½ tsp (1 g) freshly grated nutmeg
-    Salt and pepper to taste
- 1½ cups (135 g) shredded vegan cheddar cheese

GARNISH

   Chopped parsley

MAGICAL METHOD

1. In a Dutch oven with olive oil on medium-high heat, add onions along with a pinch of salt and pepper. Cook until translucent, about 6 to 7 minutes, then add the celery, carrots and another pinch of salt and pepper. Cook for 4 to 5 minutes. Add garlic, stirring until combined.

2. Set the heat to medium. Sprinkle in the dried herbs, mix, then add the vegan mince, using a spoon to break up the larger pieces. Turn the heat to medium-high and cook, stirring occasionally, for 6 to 8 minutes. Add a pinch of salt and pepper.

3. Add the thyme, rosemary and tomato paste. Stir and let cook for 3 minutes.

4. Deglaze the pan with red wine, making sure to scrape up the flavor from the bottom of the pan. Add bay leaves, star anise, cinnamon stick, liquid smoke, broth, Worcestershire sauce, maple syrup, instant coffee, lentils, a pinch of pepper, paprika, nutmeg and Marmite. Stir until combined. Cover with lid, set heat to low and cook for 30 minutes.

5. Add orange juice and zest, then mix until combined. Adjust seasoning to taste. Set aside.

6. In a large saucepan with 6 cups (1.5 liters) of cold water and a pinch of salt, add the potatoes. Set heat to medium-high and cook for 14 to 18 minutes or until fork tender. Drain, then let steam for 2 to 4 minutes.

7. Meanwhile, put the pan back on the heat. Add the oat cream and vegan butter and cook until melted, about 2 minutes. Add the cooked potatoes back to the pan and turn the heat to medium-low. Mash the potatoes until there are no lumps left. Season with mustard, nutmeg, salt and pepper. Add 1 cup (90 g) cheddar and stir until combined.

8. Preheat oven to 425 degrees F (220 degrees C).

9. In an oven-safe dish, add the filling, spreading it evenly across the bottom, then add the mashed topping, spreading evenly. Top with ½ cup cheddar and bake for 25 minutes.

10. Garnish with chopped parsley. Best enjoyed with a cold beer.

....

The Kitchen Witch is humming...
"Loved Ones and Leaving"
—*Nicholas Hooper*
....

Chicken Pie

In a scene from *Goblet of Fire*, by seven o'clock, the long dining table in the garden at the Burrow is set by Mrs. Weasley. As dishes laden with her homemade savory pie fly around the table, Harry realizes he's been living off scraps at the Dursleys' all summer. He digs in with relish.

PREP TIME 15 minutes **COOK TIME** 2 hours to overnight **YIELD** Enough for 4–6 Weasleys

INGREDIENTS
FILLING

- 1 white onion, finely diced
  Pinch of salt and pepper
- 2 celery sticks, finely diced
- 1 medium carrot, finely diced
- 2 cups (150 g) oyster mushrooms, shredded
- 1 tsp (2 g) fennel seeds
- 1 tsp (2 g) cumin seeds
- 1 tsp (2 g) nigella seeds
- 1 tsp (2 g) ground coriander
- 2 tsp (4 g) garlic powder
- 2 tsp (4 g) dried oregano
- 1 tsp (2 g) dried mango powder
- 1 tsp (2 g) ground allspice
- 2 tsp (4 g) sweet smoked paprika
- 1 tsp (2 g) dried mint
- 4 curry leaves
- 1 tsp (2 g) vegan trassi
- 8 cloves of garlic
- 1 tsp (2 g) ginger, freshly grated
- 1 Tbsp (10 g) vegan red curry paste
- 1 tsp (2 g) ssamjang
- 3 sprigs thyme
- 1 star anise
- 2 lime leaves
- 2 cardamom pods
- 1 fresh lemongrass stalk
- 1½ cups plus 2 Tbsp (320 g) vegan chicken, cut into bite-size pieces
- 1 can coconut milk
- 1 tsp (2 g) mirin
  Zest and juice of 1 lime
- 1 cup (164 g) corn
- 1 Tbsp (20 g) maple syrup
- 2 cups (268 g) frozen peas
- 1 cup (160 g) raisins

PASTRY

- 4 cups (500 g) plain flour
- ½ tsp (1 g) salt
- 2 tsp (4 g) cumin seeds
- 2 tsp (4 g) curry powder
- 1 cup and 1 Tbsp (250 g) vegan butter, chilled
- ¼ cup, plus 3 Tbsp (95 ml) cold water

MEMORY VIAL

This chicken pie is inspired by my mother's Antillean heritage. From the moment I was born, she invited me into her kitchen to look over her dainty shoulders. She brought flavor into my life, and this pie is the origin of our culture combined with the fragrance of our home: the island of spice.

COATING

2 Tbsp (30 ml) oat cream
1 tsp (5 g) maple syrup
1 tsp (2 g) sesame seeds
1 tsp (2 g) nigella seeds

GARNISH

Fresh coriander
Lime wedges

MAGICAL METHOD

1. The filling is best made the day before. In a Dutch oven with olive oil on medium-high heat, add onions and a pinch of salt and pepper and cook until translucent, about 5 minutes. Add celery and carrots. Cook for 5 minutes, stirring occasionally.

2. Add the oyster mushrooms and a pinch of salt and pepper and cook until golden brown, about 6 to 8 minutes.

3. Set the heat to medium. Stir in the dried spices, curry leaves, a dash of olive oil, vegan trassi, garlic, ginger, curry paste and ssamjang. Cook for 2 to 4 minutes.

4. Add thyme, star anise, lime leaves and cardamom. Cook for 2 minutes. Add a pinch of salt and pepper and stir until combined. With the back of a knife, bruise the lemongrass. Tear in half and add to the pan. Stir well.

5. Add vegan chicken to the pan and cook about 5 to 6 minutes, stirring occasionally, making sure to brown on all sides.

6. Stir in the coconut milk, mirin, lime zest and juice and corn. Cook for 2 to 3 minutes, then add maple syrup and season with salt and pepper. Mix well. Set heat to medium-low and cook uncovered for about 20 minutes or until most of the sauce has evaporated.

7. Mix in the frozen peas and raisins. Adjust seasoning to taste. Let cool completely.

8. Meanwhile, in a large mixing bowl, add the dry pastry ingredients.

9. Grate in the vegan butter and rub into the flour with your fingertips until the mixture resembles breadcrumbs. Make a well in the center, then gradually pour in the cold water. Knead and mix until it forms a rich dough. Do not overmix!

10. Divide the dough into two parts, one for the base and one for the lid. Flatten the dough, then wrap it in baking paper to prevent it from drying out. Refrigerate for at least 1 hour.

11. Grease the pie dish with vegan butter or olive oil. To form the pie base, place one piece of dough between two pieces of baking paper. Roll the dough to a thickness of less than 1 cm. Roll it out generously so a bit hangs over the edge of the pie dish.

12. Remove the rolled dough from the paper and place it into the pie dish, pressing firmly. Add the filling.

13. Roll out the second piece of dough the same way. Remove the paper, then place the dough atop the pie. Press down on the sides to seal. Using a fork, crimp the edges. Slice a 2-inch (5-cm) hole in the middle of the lid to vent the steam as the pie cooks.

14. Preheat the oven to 375 degrees F (190 degrees C).

15. Combine the oat cream and maple syrup, then brush over the top. Sprinkle on the sesame and nigella seeds. Bake for 50 minutes or until golden brown. Remove from oven and let cool for 15 minutes. Garnish with coriander and lime wedges. Serve alongside a fresh salad with capers on the side.

....

The Kitchen Witch is humming…
"Harry and Ginny"
—Alexandre Desplat

....

From the Kitchen Witch

Bake the pie on the bottom of the oven. Rotate at least once halfway through baking time and give the pie another coat with the pastry brush for an incredible golden brown finish.

This pie is delicious whether you make it in a round tin or a square one!

Magnificent Meatballs in Creamy Onion Sauce

Harry first visits the Burrow in *Chamber of Secrets*, where Molly Weasley is often seen cooking ample servings of hearty meals. These meatballs simmering in a creamy onion sauce are the perfect meal for welcoming a dear friend to your home.

PREP TIME 10 minutes   **COOK TIME** 45 minutes   **YIELD** Enough for 4 greeted guests

INGREDIENTS

CREAMY ONION SAUCE

- 1 Tbsp (15 ml) olive oil
- 2 Tbsp (28 g) vegan butter
- 5 white onions
- ½ cup (75 g) small pickled onions, cut into half-moons
- Salt and pepper to taste
- 6 cloves of garlic, crushed
- 1 Tbsp (10 g) fresh tarragon, finely chopped (about 3 sprigs)
- 2 tsp (4 g) fresh thyme, finely chopped (about 3 sprigs)
- 1 bay leaf
- 1 Tbsp (10 g) mixed dried Italian herbs
- 2 Tbsp (20 g) nutritional yeast
- ¼ tsp (0.5 g) ground cloves
- 1 Tbsp (10 g) Dijon mustard
- ½ cup (125 ml) vegan white wine
- 1 tsp vegan Worcestershire sauce
- 1 cup (250 ml) mushroom stock
- 1 tsp (2 g) Marmite
- 4 cups (946 ml) oat cream
- 1 tsp (2 g) freshly grated nutmeg
- Zest and juice of 1 lemon
- 2 Tbsp (16 g) parsley, finely chopped
- 3 Tbsp (30 g) chives, finely chopped

MEATBALLS

- 2½ cups (500 g) vegan mince
- 5 cloves of garlic, crushed
- 2 Tbsp (11 g) vegan Parmesan
- 1 Tbsp (10 g) breadcrumbs
- 1 tsp (5 ml) vegan Worcestershire Sauce
- 1 tsp (2 g) Dijon mustard
- Salt and pepper to taste
- ½ tsp (1 g) smoked paprika
- 1 tsp (2 g) freshly grated nutmeg
- 1 tsp (2 g) fennel seeds
- 1 tsp (2 g) dried oregano
- 1 tsp (2 g) onion powder
- 1 tsp (2 g) garlic powder
- Salt and pepper to taste
- 1 Tbsp (15 ml) olive oil
- 1½ cups plus 3 Tbsp (400 ml) frying oil

GARNISH

- 4 shallots, sliced in thin circles
- Vegan Parmesan, grated
- Chopped parsley

MAGICAL METHOD

1. In a saucepan with olive oil on medium-high heat, add the butter and cook until melted, about 1 to 2 minutes. Add white and pickled onions, stirring to coat, then add a pinch of salt and pepper. Cook for 5 to 7 minutes, stirring occasionally.

2. Set the heat to medium-low, cover with lid and let the onions cook for 10 minutes or until caramelized. Remove the lid, add garlic and stir until combined. Add tarragon and thyme, stirring until

add the meatballs one by one, being careful not to overcrowd the pan (do this in two batches if needed). Cook the meatballs on all sides for 3 to 4 minutes, turning occasionally.

9. In another large frying pan, pour in frying oil and set heat to medium-high. Gently dip the end of a wooden spoon into the oil. If the oil begins to bubble around the spoon, it's hot enough.

10. Fry the shallots in the oil for 4 to 5 minutes or until crispy and golden brown. Using tongs, remove the shallots to a plate with paper towels to drain. Sprinkle with salt.

11. Pour the sauce into a serving dish and place the meatballs on top or serve them separately. Top with fried shallots, grated Parmesan and parsley. Serve immediately.

The Kitchen Witch is humming…
"At the Burrow" —Alexandre Desplat

fragrant, about 2 to 4 minutes.

3. Add the bay leaf, Italian herbs, nutritional yeast, ground cloves and mustard. Mix until combined.

4. Set the heat to medium-high, then deglaze the pan with white wine and Worcestershire sauce, being sure to scrape the bottom. Stir until wine has evaporated, about 2 to 3 minutes.

5. Stir in the stock, Marmite, oat cream and nutmeg. Set heat to low and cook for 10 minutes.

6. Add the lemon zest and juice, parsley, chives and salt and pepper to taste. Adjust seasoning as needed. Keep on low heat until ready to serve.

7. In a large mixing bowl, add the mince, garlic, Parmesan, breadcrumbs, Worcestershire sauce, mustard, meatball spices and salt and pepper to taste. Using your hands, mix until well combined. Roll into ping pong ball-sized balls.

8. In a large frying pan with olive oil on medium-high heat, quickly

From the Kitchen Witch

This recipe is best served with a loaf of garlic bread to soak up all the amazing flavors from the creamy onion sauce. Prefer a lighter supper? These magnificent meatballs pair well with wild rice.

Heartwarming Goulash

When students from the mysterious Durmstrang Institute stay at Hogwarts in *Goblet of Fire*, their arrival sets the tone for a special dish: a wholesome bowl of a traditional goulash, plenty of magic included. This recipe is for champions and friends.

PREP TIME 10 minutes **COOK TIME** 45–50 minutes **YIELD** Enough for 4–6 fierce friends

INGREDIENTS

JACKFRUIT BEEF

- ½ cup (143 g) BBQ sauce
- 1 tsp (5 ml) olive oil
- ½ tsp (1 g) smoked paprika
- 1 tsp (2 g) garlic powder
- 1 tsp (2 g) onion powder
- Sea salt and pepper to taste
- 1 can of jackfruit, in brine

GOULASH

- 4 cups (300 g) mixed mushrooms
- Sea salt and pepper to taste
- 2 red onions, finely diced
- 3 celery sticks, cut into half-moons
- 2 medium carrots, peeled, halved, cut into half-moons
- 4 medium waxed potatoes, diced into cubes
- 1 tsp (2 g) fennel seeds
- 1 tsp (2 g) cumin seeds
- 1 tsp (2 g) nigella seeds
- 2 tsp (4 g) caraway seeds
- 1 tsp (2 g) ground cinnamon
- 1 tsp (2 g) ground coriander
- 2 tsp (4 g) smoked paprika
- 1 tsp (2 g) freshly grated nutmeg
- 1 tsp (2 g) ground cumin
- 7 cloves of garlic, crushed
- 1 tsp (2 g) fresh rosemary, finely chopped (about 1 sprig)
- 1½ Tbsp (10 g) fresh thyme, finely chopped (about 4 sprigs)
- 1 red chile, halved, deseeded, cut into thin strips
- 2 Tbsp (32 g) tomato paste
- 2 bay leaves
- 3 drops liquid smoke
- 1 Tbsp (10 g) harissa paste
- 1 tsp (5 g) grainy mustard

1 Tbsp (15 ml) dark molasses

1 Tbsp (15 ml) balsamic vinegar

2¼ cups (540 g) high-quality canned chopped tomatoes

1½ cups plus 3 Tbsp (400 ml) vegetable stock

3 red bell peppers

Zest and juice of 1 lemon

TO SERVE

4 cups (400 g) vegan noodles or pasta

6 Tbsp (84 g) vegan butter

Salt and pepper to taste

GARNISH

Fresh dill, chopped

Fresh parsley, chopped

Vegan sour cream

MAGICAL METHOD

1. In a mixing bowl, combine BBQ sauce, olive oil, smoked paprika, garlic powder, onion powder, salt and pepper, mixing well. Add the jackfruit and massage the mixture into the fruit. Refrigerate for at least 30 minutes.

2. In a Dutch oven with olive oil on medium-high heat, fry the mushrooms for 7 to 8 minutes or until caramelized. Add a pinch of salt and pepper. Remove from pan and set aside.

3. Add onions and fry until translucent, about 6 to 7 minutes. Stir in a dash of olive oil, then add celery and carrots. Cook for 10 minutes on medium-low heat.

4. On medium-high heat, add the potatoes to the Dutch oven along with a pinch of salt and pepper and cook on all sides for 6 to 8 minutes.

5. Add fennel, cumin, nigella and caraway seeds. Stir until combined. Cook for 4 minutes, then add cinnamon, coriander, paprika, nutmeg and ground cumin. Stir, scraping the bottom of the pan, and cook for 2 to 3 minutes. Stir in garlic, then add rosemary and thyme.

6. Set the heat to medium-low. Add chile, stirring well, then add tomato paste and cook for at least 3 minutes. Add bay leaves, liquid smoke, harissa paste, mustard and dark molasses and stir until combined. Deglaze the pan with balsamic vinegar, scraping the pan.

7. Stir in the fried mushrooms and canned tomatoes. Fill the can with vegetable stock and add to the pan along with a pinch of salt and pepper. Mix well. Set the heat to low and cook with the lid off for 40 minutes.

8. Rub the bell peppers in olive oil and sprinkle with salt and pepper.

9. In a grill pan on high heat, grill the peppers for about 4 to 5 minutes or until grill lines appear. Remove from pan and place in a reusable sandwich bag to let them steam in the residual heat for 10 minutes. Remove the skin, cut into strips and add to the Dutch oven.

10. Preheat oven to 390 degrees F (200 degrees C).

11. Roast the jackfruit for 25 minutes or until golden and crispy. For crispier edges, set the heat to broil on 465 degrees F (240 degrees C) after roasting and grill for 5 minutes. Add the jackfruit to the goulash, along with lemon zest and juice, then stir. Adjust to taste.

12. Cook pasta in salted water according to package instructions.

13. In a small saucepan on low heat, melt and brown the butter for about 5 to 8 minutes, shaking the pan occasionally to prevent burning. Pour the brown butter over the cooked pasta and season with salt and pepper.

14. Place each serving of pasta in a bowl with a ladle of goulash. Garnish with dill, parsley and vegan sour cream. Serve immediately.

....

The Kitchen Witch is humming…

"The Quidditch World Cup"

—*Patrick Doyle*

....

From the Kitchen Witch

Other serving options with this Heartwarming Goulash: mashed potatoes, dumplings, rice or bread.

Roasted Garden Vegetables with Silky Béchamel Sauce

After Fred, George and Ron steal the Ford Anglia to rescue Harry from Privet Drive in *Chamber of Secrets*, Harry finds himself at the Burrow, where Molly Weasley's garden provides the freshest produce imaginable: heaps of roasted, spiced greens covered in a crown of homemade béchamel.

PREP TIME 10 minutes   **COOK TIME** 1 hour 15 minutes   **YIELD** Enough for 4 witches and wizards

INGREDIENTS

BÉCHAMEL SAUCE

2¾ cups (650 ml) oat milk

2 bay leaves

3 cloves of garlic

2 spring onions, quartered

5 black peppercorns

¼ cup plus 1 Tbsp (65 g) vegan butter

1 tsp (2 g) caraway seeds

½ cup plus ½ Tbsp (65 g) plain flour

2 tsp (4 g) Dijon mustard

2 Tbsp (16 g) nutritional yeast

1 tsp (2 g) freshly grated nutmeg

1 cup (113 g) vegan grated mozzarella

2 Tbsp (11 g) vegan grated Parmesan

Salt and pepper to taste

ROASTED VEGETABLES

1 head of broccoli

½ squash

1 leek

1 head cauliflower, cut into florets

3 carrots, halved

2 bulbs of garlic, halved

3 beetroots, peeled, quartered

2 cups (300 g) mixed cherry tomatoes

2 red onions

2 sweet potatoes, unpeeled, diced into 0.75-inch (2-cm) cubes

½ cup (100 g) homemade pesto (see pg. 54)

½ cup (125 ml) olive oil

4 sage leaves

1 tsp (2 g) ground allspice

Salt and pepper to taste

GARNISH

Fresh basil leaves

Lemon zest

2 Tbsp (20 g) pumpkin seeds

2 Tbsp (20 g) pine nuts, roasted

½ cup (90 g) dried apricots, sliced into strips

¼ cup (45 g) dried cranberries

MAGICAL METHOD

1. In a small saucepan on medium-high heat, add the oat milk, bay leaves, garlic, spring onions and peppercorns. Simmer for 5 minutes, then turn the heat to low and cook for 10 minutes. Let cool to room temperature.

2. Start the vegetables. Cut off the tough part of the broccoli stem and slice into half-moons. Break off the florets and set aside.

3. Slice the squash into half-moons and in half again.

4. Slice the leek into thirds or quarters, depending on where the white part ends.

5. Preheat oven to 425 degrees F (220 degrees C).

6. In a large mixing bowl, add all the vegetables, pesto, olive oil and sage. Mix until fully coated. Season generously with allspice, salt and pepper. Transfer to a baking sheet and roast for 30 to 35 minutes, turning the vegetables over after about 15 minutes so they roast evenly.

7. Back to the béchamel. In a medium saucepan on medium-high heat, add vegan butter and cook until melted, about 1 to 1½ minutes. Add caraway seeds, cook for about 1 minute, then add flour and cook for at least 5 minutes, stirring vigorously until a paste forms. When the roux becomes darker in color, pour in the oat milk mixture one ladle at a time, whisking until fully incorporated. Turn heat to low and cook for 5 minutes.

8. Stir in the mustard, nutritional yeast, nutmeg, mozzarella and Parmesan, mixing until combined. Season with salt and pepper. Adjust seasoning to taste. Keep warm until serving time.

9. Pour the béchamel sauce over the vegetables in the oven. Set the oven to 450 degrees F (230 degrees C) and cook for 5 minutes.

10. Top the vegetables with the garnishes.

The Kitchen Witch is humming…

"Visit to the Zoo and Letters from Hogwarts" —John Williams

From the Kitchen Witch

This side dish makes for an amazing addition to a yuletide dinner.

Ernie's Sandwich

It's going to be a bumpy ride, as Harry finds out in *Prisoner of Azkaban*.
Going from one magical place to another—stretching, speeding and passing by
the long faces of London—can take a lot out of you. This delightfully crispy sandwich
could fill any bus driver's stomach for the long haul from the Muggle world to its
wizarding counterpart—or, you know, across town. Yeh, yeh, nearly there...

PREP TIME 20 minutes **COOK TIME** 10 minutes **YIELD** Enough for 4 hungry, stranded witches and wizards

INGREDIENTS

COLESLAW

- 2½ cups (175 g) red cabbage, finely sliced
- ¼ cup (50 ml) vegan coconut yogurt
- 4 dill pickles
- ¼ cup (50 ml) vegan mayonnaise
- 1 Tbsp (20 g) maple syrup
- ½ tsp (2 g) Dijon mustard
- 1 Tbsp (15 ml) pomegranate juice
  Seeds of half a pomegranate
- ¼ cup (10 g) fresh dill, diced
  Zest and juice of 1 clementine
  Pinch of salt
- ¼ cup (50 ml) apple cider vinegar
  Black pepper to taste
- ½ cup (75 g) grated apple (Granny Smith)
- 1 Tbsp (10 g) raisins

SANDWICH

- 6 slices (110 g) smoked tempeh
- 8 slices sourdough
- 6 slices (120 g) smoked tofu
- ½ cup (100 g) sauerkraut
- 1 red onion, thinly sliced
- 2 fresh figs, sliced
- ½ cup (75 g) grated purple carrot
- 6 radishes, sliced
- 1 small handful of purple sango (microgreen sprouts) or alfalfa

TEMPEH MARINADE

- 2 small drops liquid smoke
- 1 Tbsp (10 ml) vegan char siu sauce
- ½ tsp (2.5 ml) sesame oil
- ½ Tbsp (7.5 ml) light soy sauce
- ½ tsp (1 g) sambal badjak
- ¼ tsp (0.5 g) miso paste
- ½ tsp (1 g) garlic granules

MAGICAL METHOD

1. Mix coleslaw ingredients until combined and set aside to marinate. Making this the night before makes it even more flavorful—just make sure you squeeze out a little liquid before adding it to your sandwich.

2. Add tempeh and marinade ingredients to a small mixing bowl.

3. Rub each tempeh slice with the marinade and let it mingle in the fridge for at least 20 minutes, preferably overnight.

4. Toast the bread slices.

5. Time to assemble: buttered toasted bread, tempeh, tofu, coleslaw, sauerkraut, red onion, fig, carrot, radishes and purple sango, followed by more slaw and another slice of bread. Press each sandwich a little before slicing in half. Pack to go or serve immediately. Make it a triple-decker if you've got a fateful journey ahead.

The Kitchen Witch is humming...
"The Knight Bus" —*John Williams*

Butterbeer Apples,
pg. 128

Hallowe'en

The bats are fluttering around the Great Hall, and you're pretending you didn't get invited to Nearly Headless Nick's ghostly deathday party as you sit down for a spooky Hallowe'en feast. This holiday can be a scary time of year for many reasons, but for someone looking to join the festivities with plant-based dishes, you can find yourself looking paler than Moaning Myrtle if not prepared. Luckily, you can Confund your Housemates with these sweet and hearty Hallowe'en treats that'll trick even the most meat-loving Muggles.

Give Bathilda Bagshot a run for her Galleons with Bubbling Cauldron Cakes, keep visiting vampires at a distance with Slithering Snake Ravioli, bake up some dark magic that would make Lord Voldemort nervous with Dark Arts Fudge and so much more.

Celebrate the end of the First Wizarding War, get that troll out of the girls' bathroom and raise a glass to Sir Nicholas de Mimsy-Porpington—Hallowe'en is here!

Diadem Gemstone Gummies

As Harry learns in *Deathly Hallows*, Tom Riddle stole away to Albania to recover Rowena Ravenclaw's diadem and turn it into a Horcrux, defiling the artifact with dark magic on his path to becoming Lord Voldemort. Fortunately, there's no need to split your soul to enjoy these candied jewels infused with coconut notes and a bright lychee finish, a true gem among fruits.

PREP TIME 5 minutes   COOK TIME 15 minutes   YIELD 45 soul-splitting (but delicious) gems

INGREDIENTS

- 2 cups (500 ml) fresh coconut water
- 3 Tbsp (45 ml) Mogu Mogu blue nata de coco drink
- ¼ cup (50 g) granulated sugar
- 2 Tbsp (30 ml) lychee syrup
  Zest of 1 lime
- 1 tsp (2 g) coconut extract
- 1½ Tbsp (7.5 g) blue agar agar powder

MAGICAL METHOD

NOTE Place a gemstone mold in the freezer a few hours before you begin. A frozen mold will help the gummies set quickly.

1. In a medium-sized saucepan, pour in the coconut water, nata de coco drink, sugar, lychee syrup, lime zest and coconut extract. Whisk until combined. Set the heat to medium-high and cook for 2 to 3 minutes until the sugar is dissolved. Whisk in the agar agar and cook for 2 to 3 minutes until it is activated and the mixture begins to thicken.

2. Remove from heat. Pour the mixture into a large jug and let cool for 5 minutes.

3. Pour the mixture into the frozen gemstone mold, then tap the mold once or twice on the counter to get all the air bubbles out.

4. Refrigerate for 1 hour before serving.

The Kitchen Witch is humming...
"The Diadem" —Alexandre Desplat

From the Kitchen Witch

Replace the coconut water with pineapple juice or mango juice to amp up the fruity flavors.

Slithering Snake Ravioli

In *Deathly Hallows*, after the Dark Lord makes Malfoy Manor his headquarters,
his Death Eaters gather around a long dining table and watch in rapt attention as
he serves his beloved Nagini a dish consisting of a most unfortunate Muggle Studies
professor. This striped beetroot ravioli, complete with a brown butter sauce and notes of
smoky black garlic, will have your guests similarly spellbound
(but with significantly less violence). "Nagini, dinner."

PREP TIME 45 minutes   COOK TIME 30 minutes   YIELD Enough for 2–3 Death Eaters

INGREDIENTS

DOUGH (MAKES 250 G)

- 1⅓ cups plus 1 Tbsp (175 g) 00 flour
- ½ cup plus 1½ Tbsp (75 g) chickpea/gram flour
- ¼ tsp (0.5 g) sea salt
- ¼ cup plus 3 Tbsp (106 ml) spinach juice from 5 cups (150 g) spinach
- 1 Tbsp (15 ml) extra-virgin olive oil
- 2 tsp (4 g) activated charcoal, optional

FILLING

- 1 white onion, finely diced
- 6 cloves of black garlic
- 2 cups (317 g) beetroots, roasted, skins removed
- 3 sprigs fresh thyme
- ¼ tsp (0.5 g) freshly grated nutmeg
- Zest and juice of 1 lemon
- 1 tsp (2 g) dried mint
- 2 Tbsp (20 g) pistachios, finely chopped
- 1 cup (150 g) vegan feta or goat cheese
- 2 Tbsp (11 g) grated vegan Parmesan
- 2 tsp (10 g) maple syrup
- 1 tsp (5 ml) black truffle oil
- 2 Tbsp (20 g) fresh purple basil, finely chopped

BROWN BUTTER SAUCE

- ¾ cup plus 2 Tbsp (200 g) vegan butter
- 7 sage leaves
- Salt and pepper to taste

GARNISH

- Purple spinach
- Balsamic glaze
- Pistachios, chopped
- Black olives

MAGICAL METHOD

1. Preheat oven to 425 degrees F (220 degrees C).

2. In a large mixing bowl, add the dry dough ingredients. Make a well in the center, then pour in the spinach juice and olive oil. Using your hands, mix everything together until a dough forms. Dump the dough onto a large flat surface and knead until it becomes soft and pliable. To check if the dough is ready, poke it with your finger—if it springs back, move on to the next step.

3. Form the dough into a disc shape and slice in half. Wrap one half in cling wrap and place in the fridge. Knead the activated charcoal into the second half, wrap in cling wrap and place in the fridge. Refrigerate both for at least 1 hour.

4. In a frying pan with olive oil on medium-high heat, add the onions and cook until translucent, about 7 to 8 minutes. Add a pinch of salt and pepper.

5. Add the garlic. Mix until combined and turn the heat down to medium.

6. Using a box grater, finely grate the roasted beetroots. Squeeze out any remaining juice before adding the beetroots and their juice to the pan. Add a pinch of salt and pepper, thyme, nutmeg, lemon zest and juice, dried mint, pistachios and vegan feta or goat cheese and mix until combined. Season to taste with salt and pepper.

7. Add in the Parmesan, maple syrup, truffle oil and basil and stir well until everything is combined. Adjust to taste with salt and pepper. Set aside and let cool completely.

8. Set a pasta machine on its largest setting, dust it with a little pasta flour (and dust the surface you're using) and grab a friend if you can. Remove the green dough from the fridge, then roll it into a rectangle or oval shape with a rolling pin until it reaches a thickness of about 5 mm. With a friend's help, feed the dough through the machine, changing the machine to a smaller setting with each pass. After about five to six passes through the machine, the pasta should be ready to go. You should be able to see your fingers through the dough.

9. Remove the black dough from the fridge and prepare it as you did the green dough.

10. Next, set the pasta machine to the tagliatelle setting and feed the black dough through. (If your machine does not have this, cut the pasta into 1-cm strips.) Place the green rolled dough in the middle of the surface you're working on. Separate the black dough strips, then place each strand on top of the green pasta with about 2 cm between each strand. Trim the ends of the pasta to make it uniform. Apply the flat rolling attachment on the pasta machine and feed the combined pasta through the machine. Slice the pasta dough in half to create the top and bottom of the ravioli.

11. Spoon 12 dollops of ½ Tbsp filling onto the bottom sheet of dough. Make sure there's a good amount of space between each dollop. Cover the filling with the top sheet of dough. Gently press out the air from around each filling portion, then firmly press around the filling to seal the dough. Using a knife or pizza cutter, cut the portions into 12 ravioli squares. Make sure to seal the edges.

12. In a small saucepan on medium-high heat, add the butter and cook until browned, stirring frequently, about 6 to 7 minutes. During the last minute of cooking, sprinkle in the sage, salt and pepper. Set aside and keep warm until serving.

13. Fill a large saucepan with 6 to 7 cups (about 1.5 liters) of water and add a generous amount of salt. Bring to a boil, then gently add the ravioli (do this in two batches if your saucepan is not large enough). The ravioli are done when they float to the surface, about 1 to 3 minutes.

14. Add the cooked ravioli to the brown butter sauce and mix until combined, or spoon the brown butter sauce onto a plate, followed by the ravioli. Garnish. Serve immediately—or face the wrath of your hungry guests.

....

The Kitchen Witch is humming…
"Snape to Malfoy Manor"
—Alexandre Desplat
....

From the Kitchen Witch

This recipe is perfect for a spooky and moody date night!

Bubbling Cauldron Cakes

The Shrieking Shack, rumored to be the most haunted building in Britain,
is the perfect spot for a secret All Hallow's Eve celebration. All one would need are
some delicious treats to accompany the tricks. These Bubbling Cauldron Cakes,
topped with dark chocolate and crackling fire icing, should do nicely.

PREP TIME 10 minutes   COOK TIME 90 minutes   YIELD 16 cakes

INGREDIENTS

- 2 cups (500 ml) chocolate oat milk
- 2 Tbsp (30 ml) fresh lemon juice
- ⅔ cup (150 g) vegan butter, room temperature
- 2¼ cups (400 g) caster sugar
- 1 Tbsp (15 ml) vanilla extract
- 1⅔ cups plus 2 Tbsp (223 g) all-purpose flour
- 1 Tbsp (10 g) baking soda
  Pinch of salt
- ¾ cup plus 1 Tbsp (170 g) Dutch cacao powder
- 1 Tbsp (10 g) instant coffee powder
- 1 tsp (2 g) ground cinnamon
- ¼ cup plus 2 Tbsp (95 g) vegan natural cream cheese

CHOCOLATE DIP

- ¾ cup (200 g) dark chocolate (70%), finely chopped
- 2 tsp (10 ml) coconut oil
  Pinch of salt

RED ICING

- ⅓ cup plus 1 Tbsp (50 g) powdered sugar
- 1 Tbsp (10 g) beetroot powder
- 1½ tsp (6 ml) oat milk

YELLOW ICING

- ⅓ cup plus 1 Tbsp (50 g) powdered sugar
- 1 Tbsp (10 g) turmeric powder
- 1½ tsp (5 ml) oat milk
  Zest of 1 lemon

GREEN ICING

- ⅓ cup plus 1 Tbsp (50 g) powdered sugar
- 1 Tbsp (10 g) spirulina powder
- 1½ tsp (6 ml) oat milk

GARNISH

16 Cake pop sticks or Hallowe'en
   straws
   Vegan green pearl sprinkles
   Sugar eye sprinkles

MAGICAL METHOD

1. Preheat oven to 355 degrees
F (180 degrees C). Coat a
springform pan in vegan butter
then line with parchment paper.
Set aside.

2. In a large jug, add the oat
milk and lemon juice. Mix and
set aside to curdle, about 8 to 10
minutes.

3. Meanwhile, in a large mixing
bowl or stand mixer bowl, add
the butter, sugar and vanilla.
Whip on medium-high until
pale and fluffy, about 5 to 6
minutes. (If mixing by hand,
about 10 to 12 minutes.) In a
separate mixing bowl, add the
dry ingredients: flour, baking
soda, salt, cacao powder, instant
coffee and cinnamon. Mix with
a whisk until fully combined
with no lumps.

4. Set the stand mixer on low.
Using a wooden spoon, add two
spoonfuls of the dry ingredient
mixture and mix until the flour is
combined with the butter, then
add a few splashes of oat milk
and mix. Repeat these steps until
you have combined all of the dry
ingredient mixture.

5. Transfer the batter with a
spatula to the lined springform

pan and level the top with a
palette knife. Tap the pan against
the counter to release any air
bubbles. Bake for 45 minutes
until risen and fluffy. Let cool
completely.

6. Once the cake has cooled,
gently remove from the pan
and crumble it. Spoon in the
vegan cream cheese before using
your hands to mix everything
together. Roll this cake mixture
into 16 balls. Pierce each ball to
the center with a cake pop stick.
Place in the freezer for at least
20 minutes.

7. Fill a medium-sized saucepan
one-third of the way with water
and set the heat to medium-high.
Place a well-fitting heat-proof
mixing bowl on top.

8. Add the chopped chocolate
to the mixing bowl and let it
melt down for about 5 to 6
minutes, stirring occasionally,
until completely melted. Add
the coconut oil and salt, remove
from heat and set aside.

9. Remove the cake balls from
the freezer. Line a plate with
parchment paper. Dip each ball
one by one into the chocolate,
coating completely, then place
on the parchment paper with the
stick up. Refrigerate to let the
chocolate set, about 20 minutes.

10. Meanwhile, to make
the colored icings, add the
ingredients for each into three
bowls. Whisk water into each

bowl until the icing is smooth.
Transfer each to a prepared
piping bag with a piping tip.

11. Remove the cake balls from
the fridge. Using the red and
yellow icing, pipe flames in lines
from where the stick pierces
the cake pop to the middle of
the pop. Let the icing set for 5
minutes.

12. Peel the cake pops off the
parchment paper and turn them
upside down so the flattened
bottom is now on top. Stick
the cake pops into an apple,
pumpkin or decorative display
for support.

13. Gently spoon 1 tsp of
leftover chocolate on top of each
cauldron. Once that hardens,
about 10 minutes, pipe green
icing onto the flat top of each
cauldron and let rest for 5
minutes. Garnish and serve.

....

The Kitchen Witch is humming…
"Double Trouble" —John Williams
....

From the Kitchen Witch

**Transfer any leftover
chocolate dip to a piping
bag with a small tip to create
handles on the sides of the
Cauldron Cake Pops for
extra House points.**

Bellatrix's Blackberry Velvet Tart

Inspired by Lord Voldemort's fiercely devoted follower Bellatrix Lestrange, who first appears in *Goblet of Fire*, this dangerously delectable tart features an Oreo crumb base—an edible homage to the house of Black—and an ample helping of rich blackberry filling that'll have you craving Volde-more.

PREP TIME Overnight   COOK TIME 30 minutes   YIELD Enough for 6–8 members of the House of Black

INGREDIENTS

CHEESECAKE FILLING

- 1⅓ cups (200 g) cashews
- 1 tsp (5 ml) vanilla extract
- ½ cup (143 g) cream of coconut
- ½ cup (75 g) fresh or frozen blackberries
- ¼ cup (60 g) maple syrup
- Zest of 1 lemon
- ½ cup (120 g) whipped coconut cream
- ¼ cup plus 2 tsp (65 ml) coconut oil, melted

OREO BASE

- 1¾ cups plus 3 Tbsp (320 g) Oreos (28 cookies)
- ¼ tsp (0.5 g) ground cardamom
- Pinch of sea salt
- ⅓ cup plus ½ Tbsp (80 g) vegan butter
- 2 tsp (6 g) salted caramel peanut butter

GARNISH

- Fresh blackberries
- Blueberries
- Purple grapes

MAGICAL METHOD

1. In a large mixing bowl, add the cashews. Cover with slightly more than 2 cups (500ml) cold water and let soak overnight.

2. Add the cookies, cardamom and salt to a food processor. Pulse until the mixture resembles fine crumbs.

3. In a small saucepan on medium-high heat, melt the butter, about 1 to 2 minutes. Pour the butter into the food processor along with the peanut butter and mix until combined. The mixture should feel like wet sand.

4. Transfer the cookie mixture to a 13¾-by-4¼-inch (35-by-11-cm) springform pan greased with vegan butter. Use the back of a spoon to spread it evenly along the bottom and sides. Refrigerate until needed.

5. Drain and rinse the cashews.

6. In a clean blender or food processor, add the filling ingredients except for the melted coconut oil. Blend until smooth.

7. Transfer the filling to a large mixing bowl and whisk in the melted coconut oil.

8. Remove the cookie base from the fridge, then add the filling on top, spreading it out evenly. Tap the pan against the counter a few times to release any air bubbles. Refrigerate overnight.

9. Gently release from the pan when ready to serve. Garnish with blackberries, blueberries and grapes. Serve with an evil laugh.

The Kitchen Witch is humming…
"Darkness Takes Over"
—*Nicholas Hooper*

Butterbeer Apples

When Professor Quirrell interrupts Harry's first Hallowe'en feast in *Sorcerer's Stone* to gasp, "Troll—in the dungeons—thought you ought to know," Harry's only managed to help himself to a baked potato. Surely he would've loved a chance to sink his teeth into a festive fall treat like these toothsome caramel apples.

PREP TIME 10 minutes   COOK TIME 50 minutes   YIELD 8 apples

INGREDIENTS

CARAMEL

- 1 cup (225 g) vegan butter
- 1 cup (180 g) light brown demerara sugar
- 1 cup (340 g) corn syrup
- 1 can condensed coconut milk
- ¼ cup (50 ml) cream soda or ginger beer
- 1 vanilla pod
- 1 tsp (2 g) ground cinnamon
- ½ tsp (1 g) ground ginger
- ½ tsp (1 g) pumpkin spice
- ¼ tsp (0.5 g) sea salt
- 8 licorice root sticks
- 8 tart apples, like Granny Smith, cored

GARNISH

Nuts

Chocolate sprinkles

MAGICAL METHOD

Tip: The night before you make the caramel, put the apples in the fridge. The caramel sticks better when the apples are cold.

1. In a Dutch oven on medium-high heat, add butter, sugar, corn syrup, condensed coconut milk and cream soda or ginger beer. Stir until combined. Once the mixture reaches about 496.4 degrees F (258 degrees C) on a candy thermometer, let it cook for 30 to 40 minutes, stirring frequently. Remove from heat.

2. Scrape out the seeds of the vanilla pod with the back of a knife and add along with cinnamon, ginger, pumpkin spice and sea salt. Stir until combined.

3. Insert a licorice root stick into the hole of each apple.

4. Dip the apples in the caramel, coating well. Only do this once for a perfect, shiny finish.

5. Place the apples on a cutting board lined with parchment paper and let the caramel harden or add nuts and chocolate sprinkles before the caramel dries.

6. Serve on a large platter or in an oversized jack-o-lantern.

The Kitchen Witch is humming...

"Cakes for Crabbe and Goyle"
—*John Williams*

From the Kitchen Witch

If you have any leftover apples, slice them up and serve with ice cream, use them to garnish your apple pie or mix them into your magical morning porridge to start the day on a sweet note.

Dark Arts Fudge

If the Dark Lord had his way, every magical soul would've joined his dark cause. Things turned out differently, of course, but that shouldn't stop you from enjoying this refined (if ruinous) fudge. The blood red cherries, covered in the darkest of dark chocolate and laced with smoked sea salt and crushed Oreos, evoke Voldemort's vision and taste like victory.

PREP TIME 5 minutes   COOK TIME 20 minutes   YIELD 20 pieces

INGREDIENTS

- 2 cups (375 g) dark chocolate (87%), finely chopped
- ¼ cup (56 g) vegan butter
- 1 tsp (2 g) activated charcoal
- ½ cup (125 ml) condensed coconut milk
- Zest of 1 orange
- 1 tsp (2 g) gingerbread spices
- Pinch of smoked sea salt
- ½ cup (85 g) Oreos, crushed
- ¼ cup (50 g) Amarena cherries, chopped
- ½ cup (65 g) dried cranberries or sour cherries
- ¼ cup (48 g) black sesame seeds

MAGICAL METHOD

1. Line a brownie pan with parchment paper and set aside.
2. Fill a medium-sized saucepan one-third of the way with water, set heat to medium and place a well-fitting, heat-proof mixing bowl on top.
3. Add the chocolate to the mixing bowl and let it melt down for about 6 to 8 minutes, stirring occasionally, until melted.
4. Mix in the butter and activated charcoal until melted and combined. Remove from heat, then stir in the condensed coconut milk, orange zest, gingerbread spices and sea salt.
5. Transfer the chocolate mixture to the lined brownie pan. Sprinkle with crushed Oreos, cherries, dried cranberries, black sesame seeds and smoked sea salt to taste.
6. Refrigerate the mixture for at least 2 hours (best overnight).
7. Slice into squares and serve.

The Kitchen Witch is humming…
"The Locket" —Alexandre Desplat

From the Kitchen Witch

Wrap these sinfully delicious fudge squares in plastic wrap or place them in decorative jars or tins as a gift to friends on this spooky night.

Bubble-Head
Charm Tea,
pg. 156

Potions & Elixirs

Bewitching the mind and ensnaring the senses through carefully-brewed concoctions: skills all witches, wizards and magical people must master through potion-making. But you won't find any reason to stopper death (or invoke the wrath of a certain Potions professor) with these plant-based versions of your favorite wizarding world libations and refreshments.

Recall your time at the Three Broomsticks with the spiced autumnal favorite, Pumpkin Juice; bring yourself a bit of good fortune by downing a glimmering vial of Liquid Luck; and capture the attention of the one you've been eyeing from across the Great Hall with some sweet Amortentia.

Choosing to make your drinks vegan will surely help you bottle fame and brew glory in short order. These magical recipes will keep your friends talking more than a Babbling Potion!

Goblet of Fire Cocktail

Hogwarts is chosen to hold a legendary event in *Goblet of Fire*:
the Triwizard Tournament. Infused with chile pepper and thyme, this spicy brew
is not for the faint of heart. The question is: Are you the Hogwarts champion?
There's only one way to know for sure…

PREP TIME 10 minutes **COOK TIME** 30 minutes **YIELD** Enough for 4 Triwizard champions

INGREDIENTS

SPICY LEMONADE SYRUP

- 1 vanilla pod
  Peels and juice of 6 lemons
- 1 cup plus 1½ Tbsp (272 ml) filtered water
- 5 sprigs thyme
- ½ cup plus 2½ Tbsp (125 g) granulated sugar
  Pinch of salt
- ½ yellow chile pepper, halved and deseeded

RIM

- 1 Tbsp (10 g) agave syrup
- 2 tsp (4 g) chile flakes

COCKTAIL

- ½ cup (125 ml) butterfly pea flower tea
- ⅓ cup (80 ml) Three Spirit Livener

MAGICAL METHOD

1. Slice the vanilla pod in half. Scrape out the seeds with the back of a knife.

2. In a medium saucepan on medium heat, combine the lemon peels and juice, vanilla seeds and pod, water, thyme, sugar, salt and chile. Cook for 10 minutes. Let the syrup cool completely.

3. Dip the rim of a chilled glass in agave syrup followed by chile flakes.

4. Fill the cocktail shaker with ice cubes. Add the syrup to taste. Pour in the butterfly pea flower tea and Three Spirit Livener.

5. Shake vigorously for about 1 minute.

6. Pour the potion into the glass.

Garnish with a slice of lemon and a sprig of thyme.

⋯⋯⋯⋯⋯⋯⋯⋯⋯⋯⋯⋯⋯⋯⋯⋯

The Kitchen Witch is humming…
"The Goblet of Fire" —Patrick Doyle

⋯⋯⋯⋯⋯⋯⋯⋯⋯⋯⋯⋯⋯⋯⋯⋯

From the Kitchen Witch

For an extra smoky touch, add smoked sea salt or a few additional drops of liquid smoke/bitters. When peeling the lemons, steer clear of the pith—don't add it in, or the drink will be extra bitter.

Drink of Despair

While it may not bring to mind the cursed liquid awaiting any Horcrux seekers visiting Voldemort's sea cave in *Half-Blood Prince*, this mysterious, emerald-hued blend of bergamot and pepper will leave you utterly breathless. But be warned: You'll need someone to prevent you from drinking it all.

PREP TIME 5 minutes **COOK TIME** 30 minutes **YIELD** Enough for 3–4 Horcrux seekers

INGREDIENTS

BLACK TEA SYRUP

- ⅓ cup plus 1 Tbsp (95 ml) filtered water
- ¼ cup (50 g) granulated sugar
- 3 tsp (2 g) Earl Grey tea leaves
- 5–6 black peppercorns
- 2 cloves
- 1 star anise
- 1 tsp (2 g) fresh rosemary

DRINK

- 2⅓ cups plus 1 Tbsp (593 ml) of your favorite cola or cherry cola
- ¼ cup (50 ml) Seedlip Spice 94
- 2–3 drops liquid smoke
- Zest and juice of 1 lime
- 2 tsp (4 g) pearl white luster dust
- ¼ tsp (0.5 g) pandan extract

MAGICAL METHOD

1. In a medium saucepan on medium-high, combine the water, sugar, tea leaves, peppercorns, cloves, star anise and rosemary. Cook for 12 to 15 minutes, stirring occasionally. Let cool completely.

2. Fill a cocktail shaker with ice cubes. Add the syrup to taste, then add the cola, Seedlip, liquid smoke, lime zest and juice, luster dust, activated charcoal and pandan extract.

3. Shake vigorously for 2 minutes.

4. Strain the cocktail into a chilled glass (or chilled crystal goblet or abalone shell). Garnish with a sprinkle of luster dust.

....

The Kitchen Witch is humming…
"The Drink of Despair"
—*Nicholas Hooper*

....

From the Kitchen Witch

Serve with a chilled glass of water on the side to prevent extreme thirst.

Polyjuice Potion

With the Heir of Slytherin at large, it's time for a covert makeover to get to the bottom of why students keep getting Petrified. In *Chamber of Secrets*, that means the trio needs to take on the forms of Vincent Crabbe, Gregory Goyle and, well, what should have been Millicent Bulstrode. Loaded with lemongrass, kiwis, cucumbers and apples, this potion will at least have you turning into the best version of yourself.

PREP TIME 5 minutes **COOK TIME** 10 minutes **YIELD** Enough for Crabbe and Goyle (or 2 witches and wizards)

INGREDIENTS

- 1 aloe vera leaf
- 1 honeydew melon, peeled, deseeded and quartered
- 1 stalk lemongrass, quartered
- 2 limes, peeled and quartered
- 1 Asian pear, cored and thinly sliced
- 1 cucumber, diced
- 4 green kiwis, peeled and halved
- 2 Tbsp (20 g) fresh ginger, peeled and thinly sliced
- 1 cup (92 g) fennel, finely chopped
- 2 Granny Smith apples, cored, thinly sliced
- 2 cups (60 g) spinach
- ½ cup (60 g) Thai basil
- 2 cups (184 g) green grapes

GARNISH

- ¼ cup (7.5 g) fresh mint
- Lime wedges

MAGICAL METHOD

1. Cut off the prickly sides of the aloe vera.

2. Guide the knife all the way to the end and scoop the gel with a spoon from left to right.

3. Feed all the ingredients through a slow juicer.

4. Pour the juice through a sieve for a silky juice.

5. Garnish with mint and lime wedges.

The Kitchen Witch is humming…

"Polyjuice Potion" —Alexandre Desplat

From the Kitchen Witch

Enjoy this juice within a few hours for maximal nutrition, freshness and flavor.

BOOMSLANG

ANII

Polyjuice
Potion

Ingredients

Draught of Living Death

Down in the dungeons of Hogwarts Castle, in *Half-Blood Prince*, the cauldrons are simmering away as the Potions students race to claim the professor's prize—a tiny vial of Liquid Luck. The challenge: brew a decent Draught of Living Death. Thanks to the margin notes of the mysterious Half-Blood Prince in his textbook, Harry outbrews the competition and emerges victorious. Infused with Valerian tea, wormwood and lavender, this sleepy brew's a winner (that will, thankfully, not put you in a death-like state).

PREP TIME 10 minutes   **COOK TIME** 25 minutes   **YIELD** Enough for 2–3 advanced Potions students

INGREDIENTS

- 2 Tbsp (20 g) Valerian tea
- ½ cup (125 ml) blackberry juice
- 2 Tbsp (20 g) hazelnut syrup
- 1 star anise
- 1 tsp (2 g) fennel seeds
- 2 cloves
- 4 black peppercorns
- 2 slices fresh ginger
- 1 bay leaf
- 2 cardamom pods
- 2 cinnamon sticks
- ½ Tbsp (1 g) dried wormwood
- 1 tsp (2 g) culinary lavender
- Zest of 1 orange
- 1½ cups plus 2⅔ Tbsp (400 ml) evaporated coconut milk
- Pinch of smoked sea salt

MAGICAL METHOD

1. In a small mixing bowl, cover 2 Tbsp Valerian tea with 1 cup boiling water. Let steep for 6 to 7 minutes.

2. In a medium saucepan on medium-high heat, combine the tea, blackberry juice, hazelnut syrup, star anise, fennel seeds, cloves, peppercorns, ginger, bay leaf, cardamom, cinnamon sticks, dried wormwood, lavender, orange zest, evaporated coconut milk and smoked sea salt. Cook for 10 to 15 minutes. Let cool completely.

3. Pour the mixture through a sieve and discard the spices.

4. Pour into a chilled glass with ice. "Add a clockwise stir after every seventh counterclockwise stir" and...excellent. Serve.

....

The Kitchen Witch is humming...
"Living Death" —Nicholas Hooper
....

From the Kitchen Witch

Valerian, lavender and wormwood is a wonderful combination for a restful night's sleep.

Liquid Luck

In *Half-Blood Prince*, Harry downs a mouthful of Felix Felicis in order to prepare himself to recover a very important memory in the fight to defeat Lord Voldemort. Loaded with pineapple, passion fruit and yuzu, this sparkling jasmine lemonade is laced with gold luster dust and will almost certainly cause "giddiness, recklessness, and dangerous overconfidence" if taken in large quantities.

PREP TIME 10 minutes   **COOK TIME** 35 minutes   **YIELD** Enough for 4–5 Slug Club members

INGREDIENTS
GOLDEN SYRUP
- 1 pineapple, peeled and cubed
- 1 Golden Delicious apple, peeled and cubed
- 1 Asian pear, peeled and cubed
- 3 passion fruits, halved
- 1 Tbsp (10 g) fresh ginger, peeled and thinly sliced
- 1 lemon, peeled and quartered
- ½ cup (100 g) granulated sugar
- 1 tsp (2 g) turmeric powder
- ¼ cup (50 ml) yuzu juice

DRINK
- 2 cups (500 ml) Belvoir Elderflower Lemonade
- 2 Tbsp (14 g) gold luster dust

MAGICAL METHOD
1. Feed the pineapple, apple, pear, passion fruit, ginger and lemon through a slow juicer.

2. In a medium saucepan on medium-high heat, combine the freshly pressed juice, sugar, turmeric and yuzu. Cook for 10 minutes to reduce the syrup. Let cool completely.

3. Fill a cocktail shaker with ice cubes. Add the syrup to taste. Pour in the Belvoir Elderflower Lemonade and luster dust. Shake for about 1 minute.

4. Pour the potion into a chilled glass. Garnish with a sprinkle of luster dust before serving.

Best enjoyed on days when you'd really like things to work out in your favor.

The Kitchen Witch is humming...
"School!" —*Nicholas Hooper*

From the Kitchen Witch

For an extra herbal garnish, add fresh peppermint leaves or Thai basil. These herbs will bring luck and prosperity to your kitchen.

Elixir of Life

As an ancient alchemist could tell you, the Sorcerer's Stone will turn any metal into pure gold and even produce an elixir that will render its drinker immortal. While we can't promise this ruby-hued brew will make you live forever, in terms of this drink's cure-all properties, the ginger, beetroots, cherries and pomegranate seeds will imbue your body with a fortifying array of antioxidants.

PREP TIME 5 minutes **COOK TIME** 15 minutes **YIELD** Enough for 3–4 alchemists

INGREDIENTS

- 2 beetroots, peeled and quartered
- 2 blood oranges, peeled and quartered
- 2 cups cherries, destemmed and pitted
- ½ Tbsp (7 g) fresh ginger, peeled and thinly sliced
- Seeds of 2 pomegranates
- 2 red apples, cored and thinly sliced
- 2 cups strawberries, destemmed
- ½ watermelon, cubed
- 2 cups raspberries
- Edible gold luster dust, optional

MAGICAL METHOD

1. Feed all ingredients except luster dust through the slow juicer. Pour the juice through a sieve to remove the excess pulp.

2. Pour into a chilled glass (ice cubes optional). Stir in luster dust before serving.

The Kitchen Witch is humming…
"The Face of Voldemort"
—*John Williams*

From the Kitchen Witch

Add another superfood like maca or ashwagandha to the juice to give you a boost of natural energy. A true elixir of life.

Amortentia

First mentioned in *Half-Blood Prince*, Amortentia is the strongest,
most powerful love potion in the wizarding world. Its pungent aroma
varies from person to person depending on what attracts them.
This dangerously addictive blend of tart rhubarb, sweet strawberries and
rose lemonade will beguile any palate to the point of obsession.

PREP TIME 5 minutes   **COOK TIME** 30 minutes   **YIELD** Enough for 4 infatuated witches and wizards

INGREDIENTS

- 1 vanilla pod
- 4 rhubarb stalks, finely diced
- ½ cup (72 g) strawberries, destemmed and finely sliced
- 1 Tbsp (2 g) dried hibiscus tea
- Zest and juice of 2 lemons
- ½ cup (100 g) granulated sugar
- 1 Tbsp (10 g) pomegranate molasses
- 1 Tbsp (10 g) freshly grated ginger
- 3 cardamom pods
- 3 cloves
- 1 tsp (5 ml) rose water
- ½ cup (125 ml) filtered water
- 1 tsp (1 g) culinary lavender
- Heart-shaped ice cubes
- 1¾ cups plus 2 Tbsp (450 ml) rose lemonade

Dried rose petals
Edible pearl luster dust

MAGICAL METHOD

1. Slice the vanilla pod in half. Scrape out the seeds with the back of a knife.

2. In a medium saucepan on medium heat, combine the rhubarb, strawberries, hibiscus tea, vanilla pod and seeds, lemon zest and juice, sugar, molasses, ginger, cardamom, cloves, rose water, filtered water and lavender. Cook for 15 minutes, stirring occasionally. Strain to remove the spices and let cool completely.

3. Pour the love syrup into a heart-shaped glass or bottle with heart-shaped ice cubes. Top with rose lemonade and garnish with dried rose petals and luster dust.

....

The Kitchen Witch is humming…
"When Ginny Kissed Harry"
—Nicholas Hooper

....

From the Kitchen Witch

Place a charged rose quartz next to the stove to infuse this potion with more loving vibrations.

"Single-Malt Whiskey" Sour

In *Goblet of Fire*, the elegant students of the Beauxbatons Academy of Magic travel with their Headmistress, Olympe Maxime, to Hogwarts to participate in the Triwizard Tournament. To fly from the Pyrenees to Scotland, the students rely on winged horses to pull their flying carriage. Maxime informs Hagrid these magical creatures drink one thing: single-malt whiskey. Infused with tarragon syrup and topped with sparkling elderflower soda and a cloud-like dollop of whipped aquafaba, this drink will send your taste buds soaring.

PREP TIME 10 minutes   **COOK TIME** 10 minutes   **YIELD** Enough for 2 Beauxbatons students

INGREDIENTS

TARRAGON SYRUP

- ½ cup (125 ml) water
- ½ cup (100 g) granulated sugar
- 2 lime leaves
- 3 sprigs tarragon
- Zest and juice of 1 lemon

DRINK

- Zest and juice of 1 lime
- 2 drops bitters
- ½ cup (125 ml) Three Spirit Nightcap (alcohol-free elixir)
- 1 cup (250 ml) Belvoir Elderflower Lemonade
- 2 Tbsp (30 ml) yuzu juice

AQUAFABA CLOUD

- ½ cup (125 ml) aquafaba
- ½ cup (100 g) granulated sugar
- ½ tsp (0.5 ml) almond extract

GARNISH

- Chamomile flowers

MAGICAL METHOD

1. In a small saucepan on medium-high heat, combine the water, sugar, lime leaves, tarragon and lemon zest and juice. Cook for 10 to 12 minutes, stirring occasionally. Let cool completely.

2. In a large cocktail shaker, add the lime zest and juice and bitters. Add the syrup to taste, followed by the Three Spirit, Belvoir Elderflower Lemonade and yuzu juice.

3. Shake for at least 2½ minutes.

4. Using an electric mixer, whip up the aquafaba, adding the sugar gradually. Pour in the almond extract and whip until soft peaks form, about 4 to 5 minutes.

5. Pour the potion into a chilled glass. Garnish with a dollop of the whipped aquafaba and chamomile.

The Kitchen Witch is humming...
"Hogwarts' March" —Patrick Doyle

From the Kitchen Witch

Do not add ice cubes while shaking this potion—it will prevent the beautiful foam on top of the potion from forming. Quelle horreur!

Butterbeer Three Ways

From the time Harry, Hermione and Ron (separately) first travel to Hogsmeade in *Prisoner of Azkaban*, the friends hardly ever pass up a butterbeer while visiting The Three Broomsticks. Serve up foaming glasses of this beloved butterscotch brew chilled, frozen, hot, or all three—no sense in breaking up this trio. Some ginger in mine, please!

PREP TIME 5 minutes to overnight **COOK TIME** 20 minutes **YIELD** Enough for 2 witches and wizards

COCONUT BUTTERSCOTCH SAUCE
INGREDIENTS
- ½ cup (100 g) coconut sugar
- ⅔ cup plus 2 Tbsp (165 ml) canned coconut milk
- 1 Tbsp (10 g) vegan butter
- ½ tsp (1 g) ground cinnamon
- 1 tsp (2 g) ground ginger
- 1 tsp (5 ml) rum extract
- Pinch of sea salt

MAGICAL METHOD
In a medium saucepan on medium-high heat, add all sauce ingredients and cook, stirring, for 10 minutes. Let cool completely.

CHILLED BUTTERBEER
INGREDIENTS
- 1 tsp (5 ml) vegan butter
- 1 cup (250 g) vegan cream soda
- ½ cup (125 ml) ginger beer
- ¼ tsp (0.7 ml) ginger ale
- 1 Tbsp (10 g) coconut butterscotch sauce

TOPPING
- 4 Tbsp (40 g) coconut whipping cream
- 1 tsp (5 ml) vanilla extract
- 2 vegan shortbread cookies or gingersnaps, crushed

MAGICAL METHOD
1. In a small saucepan on low heat, melt the vegan butter, about 2 minutes.

2. In a large jug, whisk the cream soda, ginger beer and ginger ale

until combined.

3. Mix in the melted butter and butterscotch sauce.

4. In a small mixing bowl, add the coconut whipping cream and vanilla extract. Mix until firm peaks form, about 4 to 5 minutes.

5. Using a spatula, fold the crushed cookies into the coconut cream. Be careful not to overmix.

6. Pour the butterbeer into a chilled glass. Garnish with the whipped cream, a sprinkle of cinnamon and an extra spoonful of butterscotch sauce.

FROZEN BUTTERBEER
INGREDIENTS

- 1 cup (240 g) cream soda, for the ice cubes
  Zest of 1 lemon
- ½ cup (100 g) vegan vanilla ice cream
- ½ Tbsp (5 g) coconut butterscotch sauce
- 1 tsp (5 ml) melted vegan butter
- 1 tsp (5 ml) vanilla extract
  Pinch of sea salt

TOPPING

- 2 Tbsp (30 ml) aquafaba
- 2 Tbsp (20 g) coconut whipping cream
- ½ tsp (5 g) coconut butterscotch sauce
- ½ tsp (1 g) ground cinnamon
- ¼ tsp (1 ml) almond extract

MAGICAL METHOD

1. The night before, make cream soda ice cubes.

2. When you're ready to prepare the butterbeer, add the cream soda ice cubes, lemon zest, ice cream, butterscotch sauce, melted butter, vanilla extract and salt to a blender. Blend into a slush, about 1 to 2 minutes.

3. Pour the frozen butterbeer into a frozen glass.

4. In a small mixing bowl, combine the frozen butterbeer topping ingredients. Using an electric mixer, whip until firm peaks form, about 5 to 6 minutes on high speed.

5. Garnish the frozen butterbeer with the whipped topping and serve immediately.

HOT BUTTERBEER
INGREDIENTS

- 1 vanilla pod
- 1 cup (250 ml) almond milk
- 1 cup (250 ml) vegan cream soda
- ¼ tsp (1 ml) rum extract
- 1 Tbsp (10 g) coconut butterscotch sauce
- 1 cinnamon stick
  Freshly grated nutmeg
- 1 Tbsp (15 ml) vegan butter melted
- 2 cloves
- 1 star anise

TOPPING

- 2 Tbsp (20 g) coconut whipping cream
  Sprinkle of ground cinnamon
- 1 tsp (5 g) maple syrup

MAGICAL METHOD

1. Slice the vanilla pod in half, scraping out the seeds with the back of the knife.

2. In a medium saucepan on medium heat, combine the vanilla seeds and pod with the rest of the hot butterbeer ingredients. Cook for about 15 to 20 minutes, stirring occasionally.

3. Meanwhile, in a stand mixer bowl, whip up the cream, cinnamon and maple syrup for 5 to 6 minutes on high speed.

4. Pour the hot butterbeer through a sieve to discard the spices, then transfer to a large mug.

5. Spoon on the cream and garnish with a beautiful cinnamon stick or star anise.

....

The Kitchen Witch is humming...
"Harry in Winter" —*Patrick Doyle*
....

From the Kitchen Witch

Keep the corks of the butterbeer bottles to fashion into a charming necklace, which may or may not help ward off Nargles.

Pumpkin Juice

As the students hunt down drinks at the Yule Ball in *Goblet of Fire* before dancing the night away, it's easy to imagine young wizards queuing up for their fill of frosted pumpkin juice while watching the Weird Sisters take to the stage. Infused with star anise, cloves, vanilla and pumpkin spice and thickened to perfection with apricots and mango, this drink is sure to help you keep your cool as you let your hair down and get your feet off the ground.

PREP TIME 10 minutes **COOK TIME** 45 minutes **YIELD** Enough for 4¼ spooky gourds aka 4¼ cups (1 L)

INGREDIENTS

- 1 butternut squash, peeled, halved and deseeded
- Zest and juice of 1 orange
- 2 tsp (4 g) ground cinnamon, divided
- Pinch of salt
- 5 Jonagold apples, cored and thinly sliced
- 8 fresh apricots, halved and pitted
- 2 Tbsp (20 g) fresh ginger, peeled and thinly sliced
- 1 orange, peeled and quartered
- 2 cups (500 ml) water, if needed
- 1 vanilla pod
- ½ cup (100 g) granulated sugar
- 1 star anise
- 3 cloves
- 1 Tbsp (10 g) pumpkin spice
- Pinch of salt
- ⅓ cup plus 3 Tbsp (100 ml) Alphonso mango puree

MAGICAL METHOD

1. Preheat oven to 390 degrees F (200 degrees C).

2. Dice half the squash into 0.7-inch (2-cm) cubes. Line a baking sheet with parchment paper.

3. In a large mixing bowl, add diced squash, zest and juice of 1 orange, 1 tsp of ground cinnamon and a pinch of salt. Mix until combined. Transfer to the lined baking sheet.

4. Roast for 25 to 30 minutes. Let cool completely.

5. Finely slice the remaining squash half.

6. Feed the apples, apricots, ginger, orange quarters and squash through a juicer. If the juicer is having trouble running the squash through, pour in the 2 cups of water.

7. Slice the vanilla pod in half and scrape out the seeds with the back of the knife.

8. In a medium pan on medium-low heat, combine the fresh juice, vanilla seeds and pod, sugar, star anise, cloves, pumpkin spice, pinch of salt and mango puree. Mix until combined and cook for 25 minutes, stirring occasionally.

9. Either serve hot or let cool completely and serve over ice.

The Kitchen Witch is humming…
"Do the Hippogriff"
—*Jason Buckle and Jarvis Cocker*

From the Kitchen Witch

To make it fizz, add half the juice to a glass and top off with Sanpellegrino Aranciata Rossa.

Bubble-Head Charm Tea

Sure, Cedric Diggory uses the Bubble-Head Charm to rescue Cho Chang from the clutches of the merpeople in *Goblet of Fire*. What we can't conclusively determine is what Cedric does between that victory and the moment Harry emerges from the Great Lake with Gabrielle Delacour and Ron. All we know for sure is that this delightful passion fruit boba tea will make you feel like a champion.

PREP TIME 5 minutes   **COOK TIME** 45 minutes   **YIELD** Enough for 2–3 Triwizard champions

INGREDIENTS

SYRUP

- 1   stalk lemongrass
- ½   cup (100 g) granulated sugar
- ½   cup (125 ml) filtered water
- 1   tsp (5 ml) vanilla extract
- 1   tsp (5 ml) coconut or passion fruit extract
-     Zest and juice of 1 lime
- 1   lime or pandan leaf

BOBA PEARLS

- 10   cups (2.3 L) filtered water
- 1   cup (128 g) white, colored or black tapioca pearls

BUBBLE TEA

- 1   cup (250 ml) filtered water
- 2   Tbsp (2 g) dried blueberry tea
- ½   cup (2 g) butterfly pea flower tea petals
- 1   white dragon fruit, halved
- ¼   cup (50 ml) condensed coconut milk
- ½   cup (125 ml) evaporated coconut milk
- ½   cup (95 g) blueberries
- ½   cup (59 g) nata de coco

MAGICAL METHOD

1. Using the back of a knife, bruise the lemongrass to release more flavor.

2. In a small saucepan on medium-high heat, combine all syrup ingredients. Cook for at least 10 minutes, stirring occasionally. Remove the lime leaf and lemongrass. Let cool completely.

3. In a large saucepan on medium-high heat, bring the water to a simmer. Add the tapioca pearls and cook for about 4 to 5 minutes. Strain the pearls, then run them under cold water and transfer to the cooled syrup. Mix until combined and set aside.

4. In a small saucepan with water on low heat, add the blueberry tea and butterfly pea flower tea petals. Steep for 6 to 8 minutes. Strain and let cool completely.

5. Using a melon baller, scoop out the dragon fruit seeds.

6. In a small mixing bowl, whisk together the condensed coconut milk and evaporated coconut milk until smooth.

7. In a large glass, layer 2 Tbsp boba pearls, followed by the fruit and nata de coco, ice cubes, tea and condensed milk mixture. Garnish with butterfly pea flower petals. Enjoy with a boba straw.

....

The Kitchen Witch is humming...
"Moaning Myrtle" —John Williams

....

From the Kitchen Witch

For even more flavor, swap out the ice cubes for a few scoops of coconut sorbet.

Arthur's Eggnog

Does Arthur Weasley offer everyone a nightcap to distract Fleur from commenting on Celestina Warbeck's warbling broadcast in *Half-Blood Prince*? Possibly. Singing witches aside, consuming this silky, festive beverage is sure to keep even the most opinionated guests contentedly quiet, a true yuletide miracle. Bottoms up!

PREP TIME 12–24 hours for soaking **COOK TIME** 10 minutes **YIELD** Enough for 4 Weasleys

INGREDIENTS

- ¾ cup plus 1⅓ Tbsp (200 g) cashews
- 2 cups plus 1½ Tbsp (522 ml) almond milk
- ¼ tsp (0.5 g) nutmeg, freshly grated
- 1 tsp (2 g) ground cinnamon
- 3 cloves
- 1 cinnamon stick
- 1 tsp (2 g) gingerbread spices
- Pinch of salt
- ¼ cup (60 g) maple syrup
- 1 tsp (5 ml) vanilla extract
- 1 tsp (5 ml) coconut extract
- Natural yellow food coloring (for an authentic eggnog look), optional
- ½ cup (65 g) vegan white chocolate, chopped
- 1 tsp (5 ml) rum extract (alcohol free)

RIM

- Agave or maple syrup
- Crushed cookies of choice

TOPPINGS, OPTIONAL

- Whipped coconut cream
- Ground cinnamon or cinnamon stick
- Chopped hazelnuts
- Candied kumquats

MAGICAL METHOD

1. Soak the cashews in cold water overnight for the silkiest texture. Otherwise, boil the cashews for 30 minutes or soak in hot water for 2 hours.

2. In a blender, add the cashews, almond milk, spices, syrup, extracts and food coloring. Blend until smooth and creamy, about 2 to 3 minutes (or 5 minutes if using an immersion blender).

3. In a medium saucepan on medium-low heat, whisk to combine the blended cashew mixture with the white chocolate. Adjust seasoning to taste. Adding a pinch of salt will bring out the complexity of the flavors.

4. Whisk in the rum extract. Pour the mixture into a flask or bottle and let cool completely. Place in the fridge to chill for at least 6 hours, preferably overnight.

5. Dip the rim of a glass in agave or maple syrup, then coat the rim with crushed cookies. Pour the eggnog into the glass. Serve ice cold with a generous dollop of whipped coconut cream and garnish with a sprinkle of cinnamon.

The Kitchen Witch is humming…
"Christmas at Hogwarts"
—*John Williams*

MEMORY VIAL

This recipe is inspired by my amazing dad. We both have an insatiable sweet tooth and enjoy a good eggnog on Christmas Eve. Our unbreakable bond is sealed by this silky smooth drink that is always a festive fixture in our home during the holidays.

Mini Lemon
Meringue Pies,
pg. 176

Enchanting Desserts

Throw on your gloves and put on your coziest hat because we are going to leave the warmth of Hogwarts Castle and venture into the village of Hogsmeade.

While the elves down in the Hogwarts kitchens can conjure up some magical desserts of their own, nothing can beat the sugary confections found in Honeydukes! Enjoy our dairy-free rendition of Chocolate Frogs—if you can keep them from hopping away first. Or set off a detonation of flavor with vegan Exploding Bonbons and keep warm on that chilly walk back to your common room with warm and flaky Pumpkin Pasties.

All of these tasty treats can be found in the wizarding world and are now yours to enjoy in their plant-based iterations. Just be sure Filch doesn't catch you sneaking back into the castle out of old Gunhilda's hump.

Mince Pies

For Christmas during Harry's third year at Hogwarts in *Prisoner of Azkaban*, Mrs. Weasley characteristically treats him as a member of the family, sending him a scarlet jumper with the Gryffindor lion knitted on the front as well as a dozen home-baked mince pies and other treats. You can replicate the traditional flavors of this classic British dish with vegan ingredients.

PREP TIME 20 minutes   COOK TIME 1 hour 15 minutes   YIELD 12–16 mince pies

INGREDIENTS

DOUGH

- 3¼ cups (400 g) all-purpose flour
- ½ cup (90 g) light brown sugar
- ½ tsp (1 g) gingerbread spices
  Pinch of salt
- ¾ cup plus 2 Tbsp (200 g) cold vegan butter, cubed
- 2 Tbsp (30 ml) Grand Marnier
  Zest and juice of 1 orange

MINCEMEAT FILLING

- 1 cup plus 1 Tbsp (250 ml) cherry brandy
- 1 vanilla pod
- 1 cup (180 g) dark demerara sugar
- 6 Medjool dates, deseeded, finely sliced
- ¾ cup (123 g) dried cranberries
- ½ cup (65 g) fresh cranberries
- ¾ cup (100 g) raisins
- 1 Tbsp (15 ml) stem ginger in syrup, chopped
- 1 Bramley apple, peeled, finely sliced

- 1 tsp (5 ml) orange blossom water
- 1 tsp (2 g) allspice
- 1 tsp (2 g) gingerbread spices
- 1 tsp (2 g) ground cinnamon
- 1 cinnamon stick
- 1 star anise
- ¼ tsp (0.5 g) ground cardamom
  Pinch of salt
  Zest and juice of 2 clementines
  Zest of 1 lemon
- ½ cup (75 g) pistachios, finely chopped
- ½ cup (75 g) walnuts, finely chopped
- ½ cup (75 g) almonds, finely chopped

PASTRY COATING

- 2 Tbsp (30 ml) oat milk
- 1 Tbsp (20 g) maple syrup

GARNISH

  Icing sugar
  Dried cranberries

MAGICAL METHOD

1. In a large mixing bowl, combine the dry dough ingredients with a fork.

2. Mix the vegan butter into the dry ingredients until fully incorporated. Add Grand Marnier and orange zest and juice, then mix. Do not overmix or pastry will not be crisp.

3. Divide the dough in two pieces and wrap individually in cling wrap. Refrigerate for at least 1 hour.

4. Meanwhile, start the filling by pouring the brandy into a large saucepan on medium-high heat. Slice the vanilla pod in half, scrape out the seeds with the back of a knife and add pod and seeds to the pan. Add the sugar, stirring until it dissolves.

5. Add the dates, dried and fresh cranberries, raisins and stem ginger. Mix until combined. Add apple, orange blossom water, dried spices, clementine zest and juice and lemon zest, stirring well.

6. Set the heat to low. Let the mixture bubble away uncovered for 10 minutes.

7. Stir in the pistachios, walnuts and almonds. Let the mixture cool completely and remove pod.

8. Preheat oven to 355 degrees F (180 degrees C). Remove the dough from the fridge. Grease a muffin pan. Unwrap the dough and place each half on a sheet of parchment paper. Cover the dough with another piece of parchment paper, then roll the dough to a thickness of about 0.2 inches (0.5 cm).

9. Using cookie cutters, cut circles from one of the pieces of dough and stars from the other.

10. Place the dough circles in the pan and gently press down to ensure there are no air pockets. Add 1½ tsp of filling into each well, pressing down gently. Top each well with a star.

11. In a small bowl, combine the oat milk and maple syrup. Brush each pie with the mixture.

12. Bake for 20 to 22 minutes until golden brown and crisp. Let cool slightly before garnishing with icing sugar and cranberries.

....

The Kitchen Witch is humming…
"Christmas at Hogwarts" —*John Williams*

....

Apple Pie

During the start-of-term feast in *Sorcerer's Stone*, Harry watches the remnants of the main course fade away on everyone's platters, only to be magically replaced with mounds of scrumptious-looking desserts, including apple pies. These buttery, cinnamon-laced pastries are bound to make anyone feel right at home.

PREP TIME 15 minutes   **COOK TIME** 2 hours   **YIELD** Enough for 6–8 witches and wizards

INGREDIENTS

VEGAN CUSTARD

- 1⅔ cups plus 2 Tbsp (450 ml) almond milk, divided
- 2 Tbsp (20 g) cream of coconut
- 1 vanilla pod
- ½ cup (100 g) granulated sugar
- ¼ tsp (0.5 g) almond extract
- ½ tsp (1 g) turmeric powder
- Zest of 1 lemon
- 4 Tbsp (30 g) cornstarch

ALMOND FILLING

- 1½ cups (300 g) vegan almond marzipan
- 2 Tbsp (20 g) apple sauce
- Zest and juice of 1 lemon

DOUGH

- 4 cups (500 g) all-purpose flour
- 2 tsp (4 g) fennel seeds
- ½ cup plus 2 Tbsp (125 g) granulated sugar
- Pinch of sea salt
- 1 tsp (2 g) ground cinnamon
- 1 cup plus 2 Tbsp (250 g) chilled vegan butter, cubed
- 3 Tbsp (45 ml) cold water

APPLE FILLING

- 4 Granny Smith apples, peeled, cored and thinly sliced
- 4 Santana apples, peeled, cored and thinly sliced
- 1 star anise
- 1 vanilla pod
- Zest and juice of 1 lemon
- Zest and juice of 1 orange
- 1 cinnamon stick
- 2 bay leaves
- 2 cardamom pods
- 2 tsp (4 g) gingerbread spices
- 2 Tbsp (43 g) maple syrup
- ⅓ cup plus 1½ Tbsp (75 g) light brown sugar
- 2 Tbsp (20 g) stem ginger in syrup
- 1 cup (165 g) raisins
- Pinch of salt

PASTRY COATING

- 1 Tbsp (15 ml) almond milk
- 2 tsp (10 g) maple syrup

MAGICAL METHOD

1. In a medium saucepan on medium-high heat, pour in the 1⅔ cups almond milk and 2 Tbsp cream of coconut. Slice the vanilla pod in half, then scrape out and add the seeds. Whisk in the sugar, almond extract and turmeric powder, then add the lemon zest. Bring the mixture to a simmer.

2. In a small mixing bowl, add the 2 Tbsp of milk and the cornstarch, whisking until it forms a paste. Whisk into the simmering almond milk, turn the heat to low and let the mixture cook for at least 6 to 8 minutes, stirring occasionally until slightly thickened.

3. Transfer the custard mixture to a shallow container and cover with cling wrap (to prevent a skin forming on top). Let cool completely and set aside or refrigerate until needed.

4. To make the almond filling, break up the marzipan in a medium mixing bowl and spoon in the apple sauce. Add the lemon zest and juice. Mix until combined and set aside.

5. In a large mixing bowl, add

the dry pastry ingredients: flour, fennel seeds, sugar, salt and cinnamon. Mix with a fork until combined.

6. Mix the chilled vegan butter into the dry ingredients until fully incorporated. Pour in the water, then mix and knead until the dough forms.

7. Divide the pastry into two pieces, then wrap each piece in cling wrap and let rest for at least an hour in the fridge.

8. In a medium saucepan on medium heat, add the apple slices followed by the rest of the filling ingredients. Stir until combined, then cook uncovered for 10 to 15 minutes. Transfer to a large plate and let cool completely. Remove the cinnamon sticks, star anise and bay leaves.

9. Grease tart pan with vegan butter.

10. Preheat the oven to 355 degrees F (180 degrees C).

11. Whisk the almond milk and maple syrup together for the pastry coating.

12. Roll out the first half of the pastry for the bottom.

13. Spread a little flour on the kitchen surface or place the pastry between two pieces of parchment paper. Roll out to 0.2 inches (0.5 cm) thick. Carefully transfer the dough to the pan, tuck in the sides and cut off excess hanging dough.

14. Make sure each filling is cool before assembling the pie. Spread on the almond marzipan filling evenly with the back of a spoon.

15. Remove the cling wrap from the custard and stir again with a spoon or spatula. Spread it evenly on top of the almond marzipan filling.

16. Layer on the apple filling. Roll out the second piece of dough to the same thickness and place it on the pie. (Optional: Cut moons out of the dough to place on top of the pie as pictured.) Make sure there is a hole in the middle for the steam to escape.

17. Brush on the coating with a pastry brush.

18. Bake on the bottom of the oven for 50 minutes until golden brown.

19. Let cool for at least 15 minutes before diving in.

....

The Kitchen Witch is humming...
"Introducing Colin" —*John Williams*

....

Snowy Yule Log

Nobody does Christmas tradition quite like Hogwarts, and there are
few things more evocative of holidays of yore than the yule log.
Our version might not burn for 12 days, but it could fill you up for that long!

PREP TIME 10 minutes **COOK TIME** 90 minutes **YIELD** Enough for 6–8 witches and wizards

INGREDIENTS

YULE LOG

- ⅓ cup (80 ml) aquafaba
- ⅔ cup plus 1 Tbsp (175 ml) coconut milk
- 1 tsp (5 ml) fresh lemon juice
- 1⅓ cups plus 1 Tbsp (175 g) cake flour
- ½ cup plus 2 Tbsp (125 g) granulated sugar
- ¼ tsp (0.5 g) ground cardamom
- 1 tsp (2 g) gingerbread spices
  Pinch of salt
- ⅓ cup (40 g) cornstarch
- ½ tsp (1 g) baking soda
- 2 tsp (4 g) baking powder
- ¼ cup (16.5 g) shredded coconut
  Zest of 1 lime
- ¼ cup (56 g) vegan butter

FILLING

- 1 cup (240 g) whipped coconut cream
- ½ cup (120 g) vegan natural cream cheese, room temperature
- ½ cup (125 g) Amarena cherries, chopped
  Zest of 1 clementine
- 1 Tbsp (10 g) stem ginger, chopped
- 1 Tbsp (20 g) maple syrup
- 1 tsp (5 ml) vanilla extract
- ¼ tsp (0.5 g) pistachio extract

WHITE BUTTERCREAM

- ¼ cup plus 2 Tbsp (80 g) vegan white chocolate
- ⅔ cup (150 g) vegan butter, room temperature
- ½ cup (60 g) icing sugar
- 1 tsp (5 ml) vanilla extract
  Zest and juice of 1 lime
- 1 Tbsp (15 ml) vegan Baileys or Licor 43
  Pinch of salt

MARZIPAN MUSHROOMS

- 1 cup plus 1 Tbsp (250 g) white almond marzipan
- ¼ tsp (0.5 g) cacao powder, for dusting

TOPPINGS

- ½ cup (46 g) coconut flakes
  Shaved vegan white chocolate
- 2 Tbsp (15 g) icing sugar

MAGICAL METHOD

1. Preheat oven to 355 degrees F (180 degrees C).

2. Grease a 9-by-13-inch (22.8-by-33-cm) silicone Swiss Roll mold with vegan butter and line with parchment paper. Set aside.

3. In a large mixing bowl, whip the aquafaba to stiff peaks, about 5 to 6 minutes if using a stand mixer on high speed or 10 to 12 minutes if whipping by hand. Set aside.

4. In a large jug, combine the milk and lemon juice, mixing well. Set aside and let curdle for at least 10 minutes.

5. In a large mixing bowl, add the flour, sugar, cardamom, gingerbread spices, salt, cornstarch, baking soda, baking powder, shredded coconut and lime zest. Mix until combined.

6. Melt the vegan butter, then let it cool to room temperature. Fold the curdled milk and melted butter into the aquafaba until the mixture is just combined (do not overmix).

7. Using a stand mixer, set the speed to low and gradually pour the dry ingredients into the aquafaba mixture until light and fluffy. Do not overmix! Transfer the mixture to the lined baking mold, spreading evenly.

8. Bake for 15 minutes, until a toothpick inserted into the cake comes out clean. Let cool for 3 minutes.

9. Meanwhile, sift icing sugar over a clean kitchen towel (to prevent the cake from sticking).

10. Carefully turn the cake mold upside down onto the sugared tea towel but do NOT remove the parchment paper. Use a knife to trim off the rough edges of the yule log (or skip this skep if you'd prefer your finished product to have a rustic look).

11. Roll the cake into a tight cylinder. Set aside to cool completely.

12. In a large mixing bowl, whip the coconut cream until stiff peaks form, about 4 to 5 minutes.

13. Add the cream cheese and whip or mix for another 2 to 3 minutes. Next, add the cherries, clementine zest, stem ginger, maple syrup, vanilla extract and pistachio extract, mixing until combined. Refrigerate until needed.

14. Using the double boiler method described on pg. 187, melt the vegan white chocolate and let it cool completely.

15. In a large mixing bowl, add the vegan butter. Set mixer to medium-high speed and beat until pale and fluffy, 6 to 7 minutes, or about 10 to 15 minutes if whipping by hand.

16. Set the speed on low and add the icing sugar. Mix until smooth. Add the vanilla extract, lime zest and juice, Baileys or Licor 43 and salt. Mix until combined.

17. Unroll the cake, then remove the paper. Spread the filling evenly onto the cake using a spatula or palette knife, leaving a gap of about 1 cm along the edges (or else the filling will seep out of the sides once you roll the cake back into a log).

18. Roll up the cake again as tightly as possible, then transfer onto a serving platter. Using a palette knife, spread the buttercream over the log roughly (to resemble bark). You can also use a fork to add extra detail.

19. Refrigerate the cake for 10 minutes.

20. Meanwhile, shape the marzipan into small mushrooms. Dust them with cacao powder.

21. Remove the cake from the fridge. Sprinkle with coconut flakes, shaved white chocolate and icing sugar. Arrange the mushrooms on the top and sides of the cake and serve.

....

The Kitchen Witch is humming...
"Potter Waltz" —Patrick Doyle
....

From the Kitchen Witch

This recipe makes a perfect centerpiece dessert for your Yuletide dinner party!

Treacle Tart

First spotted at the start-of-term feast in *Sorcerer's Stone*, this is Harry's favorite tart: a giant, sticky piece of golden syrupy goodness served with the biggest dollop of vegan sour cream. Easily the most delicious way to end a day full of brewing potions, studying charms and practicing Quidditch.

PREP TIME 10 minutes   **COOK TIME** 1 hour 15 minutes   **YIELD** Enough for 6–8 witches and wizards

INGREDIENTS

BASE

- 4 cups (450 g) ginger nut biscuits
- 2 tsp (4 g) ground cinnamon
- Pinch of sea salt
- ½ cup plus 1 Tbsp (125 g) vegan butter

TREACLE FILLING

- 2 cups (200 g) sourdough breadcrumbs (Half a loaf of sourdough bread)
- Zest of 1 orange
- Zest of 1 lemon
- 1 cup plus ½ Tbsp (350 g) golden syrup
- 1 tsp (5 ml) vanilla extract
- ¾ cup plus 2 Tbsp (300 g) maple syrup
- 1 tsp (2 g) ground ginger powder
- 2 tsp (4 g) fresh thyme
- Pinch of sea salt
- 2 Tbsp (30 ml) apple sauce
- 2 Tbsp (20 g) orange marmalade

TOPPING

- 1 cup (150 g) roasted pecans

PASTRY COATING

- 1 Tbsp (15 ml) almond milk
- 1 tsp (5 g) maple syrup

VEGAN SOUR CREAM

- 1 cup (240 g) oat sour cream
- Zest and juice of 1 lemon
- 2 tsp (10 g) maple syrup

MAGICAL METHOD

1. Generously grease a tart pan with vegan butter. Set aside.

2. Add the cookies, cinnamon and salt to a food processor. Blend until finely crumbled.

3. In a small saucepan on medium-high heat, melt the vegan butter for about 2 to 3 minutes. Let cool slightly, then pour into the cookie mix. Pulse until the mixture resembles wet sand.

4. Transfer the cookie mix to the pan. Use the back of a spoon to press the mixture into the bottom. Refrigerate until needed.

5. Preheat oven to 355 degrees F (180 degrees C).

6. In a clean food processor, blend about half a loaf of sourdough into a fine crumb, then transfer to a large mixing bowl. Add orange and lemon zests, golden syrup, vanilla extract, maple syrup, ground ginger, thyme, sea salt, apple sauce and orange marmalade. Mix until combined.

7. Evenly spread the filling in the chilled pan. Next, arrange the pecans along the border of the tart.

8. Mix the almond milk and maple syrup. Baste the top of the tart with the mixture to prevent it from burning.

9. Bake for 40 to 45 minutes or until golden brown and set.

10. Meanwhile, in a small mixing bowl, add the oat cream, lemon zest and juice and maple syrup, stirring until combined.

11. Let the tart cool completely before serving. Garnish with a dollop of vegan sour cream and serve with a cup of strong English tea.

....

The Kitchen Witch is humming…
"Harry's Wondrous World"
—John Williams

....

From the Kitchen Witch

You can swap out thyme for another hard herb like rosemary or sage, either of which pairs well with the caramel notes of the golden and maple syrups.

Petunia's Sugared Pudding

When Aunt Petunia whips up a decadent pudding covered in violets to impress
Mr. and Mrs. Mason in *Chamber of Secrets*, she can't imagine that just a short time later
it will levitate before crashing to the floor and splattering the walls (thanks, Dobby).
A few bites of this sumptuous lime and lavender meringue will have you
floating on cloud nine—no magic required.

PREP TIME 10 minutes   **COOK TIME** 4½ hours   **YIELD** Enough for 6 bad relatives

INGREDIENTS

MERINGUE

- 1½ cups plus 1 Tbsp (375ml) aquafaba, chilled
- 1¼ cups (250 g) granulated sugar
- 1 tsp (5 ml) white wine vinegar
- 1 tsp (5 ml) vanilla extract
- ½ Tbsp (5 g) cream of tartar or cornstarch
- Pinch of salt

VIOLET WHIPPED CREAM

- 1⅔ cups (400 ml) coconut cream
- 1½ Tbsp (16 g) Klop-Fix
- 2 tsp (4 g) dried blueberry powder
- 1 tsp (5 ml) vanilla extract
- 1 tsp (5 ml) lavender syrup
- Zest of 1 lemon

GREEN WHIPPED CREAM

- 1⅔ cups (400 ml) coconut cream
- 1½ Tbsp (16 g) Klop-Fix
- 5 drops pandan extract
- 1 tsp (5 ml) vanilla extract
- Zest of 1 lime

GARNISH

- ½ cup (200 g) maraschino cherries
- 10–13 purple edible violets
- 10–13 purple chamomile flowers

MAGICAL METHOD

1. You will need four baking sheets lined with parchment paper. Using a pencil, draw a 7.8-inch (20-cm) circle on three of the sheets and a 9.4-inch (24-cm) circle on the other sheet. Set aside. Preheat oven to 355 degrees F (180 degrees C).

2. In a large mixing bowl or stand mixer bowl, whisk the chilled aquafaba on high speed for 7 to 8 minutes or until soft peaks form. Add the sugar one spoonful at a time, then add the vinegar. The mixture will turn glossy.

3. Add the vanilla extract and mix again. Sift in the cornstarch, add salt and mix until combined.

4. Transfer the meringue to a prepared piping bag with a medium round nozzle tip.

5. Starting from the outer edges, pipe a thick ring of meringue inside the circles. Work in a spiral shape, ending at the center of the circle. Place the meringues in the oven at 230 degrees F (110 degrees C) and bake for 2 hours. Note: DO NOT OPEN THE OVEN. Let cool completely in the oven.

6. Meanwhile, in a large mixing bowl, add the coconut cream from the violet and green whipped cream recipes. Whip on high speed until stiff peaks form, about 7 to 8 minutes. Add the Klop-Fix while the mixer is running to stabilize the cream. Divide the cream into two bowls.

7. In one bowl, combine the blueberry powder, vanilla, lavender syrup and lemon zest. In the other bowl, combine the pandan, vanilla and lime zest. Add each cream to a prepared piping bag with a star nozzle.

8. Remove the meringues from the oven and carefully peel off the paper.

9. Place a dollop of whipped cream in the center of a serving platter, then add the 9.4-inch (24-cm) meringue circle. Starting from the outside, pipe a layer of the green whipped cream, working in a spiral and ending at the center.

10. Next, place one of the three smaller meringue circles on top. Pipe violet cream on top of this layer the same way. Repeat this again for the second small circle, but leave the top meringue layer plain (for now).

11. Pipe green whipped cream roses all along the bottom, then pipe purple whipped cream roses on the top layer and in between the meringue layers. Place a cherry on top of each rose and add flowers as you like.

NOTE: Meringue-based desserts are best enjoyed right away and cannot sit for long.

TIP: Adding the vinegar at the beginning stage of whipping really helps with the volume.

The Kitchen Witch is humming…
"Dobby the House Elf"
—*John Williams*

Full Moon Cookies

Harry doesn't see the inside of Ravenclaw Tower until *Deathly Hallows*, as he searches for the diadem Horcrux. After entering the tower's circular common room, he notices a ceiling covered in stars....

PREP TIME 5 minutes   COOK TIME 45 minutes–1 hour   YIELD 25 cookies

INGREDIENTS

- 1 Tbsp (15 ml) moon water, chilled
- 1 cup plus 2 Tbsp (250 g) vegan butter, room temperature
- 1 cup (200 g) granulated sugar
  Zest of 1 orange
  Zest of 1 lemon
  Zest of 1 lime
- 1 Tbsp (15 ml) vanilla extract
- ¼ tsp (0.5 g) almond extract
- 2 tsp (4 g) fresh tarragon, finely chopped
- 2 cups (250 g) all-purpose flour
- 1 Tbsp (10 g) poppy seeds
- 2 tsp (4 g) culinary lavender
  Pinch of sea salt

TOPPINGS

Golden edible luster dust
Blue edible glitter

MAGICAL METHOD

1. On the night of a full moon, cleanse a 16-oz (500-ml) bottle by wafting it with your favorite incense. Fill the bottle with clean water and place it directly in the moonlight to absorb the moon's energy for several hours, preferably overnight. Retrieve the bottle before sunrise.

2. In a large mixing bowl or stand mixer bowl, add the vegan butter and sugar. Mix on medium-high speed until pale and fluffy, around 6 to 7 minutes.

3. Add the orange, lemon and lime zests, vanilla and almond extracts and tarragon, then mix well. Set mixer to low speed and gradually add the flour. Sprinkle in the poppy seeds, culinary lavender and salt. When everything is incorporated, pour in the moon water.

4. Transfer the cookie dough onto a flat surface lined with parchment paper. Roll the dough into a thick sausage, wrap in parchment paper and refrigerate for 1 hour.

5. Roll out the dough to a thickness of about 1 cm. Cut out the cookies using a moon cookie cutter, then place in the freezer for at least 30 minutes to prevent the cookies from losing their shape.

6. Preheat oven to 355 degrees F (180 degrees C).

7. Bake the cookies for 12 to 15 minutes or until golden brown on top. Let cool completely.

8. Coat in gold luster dust and blue glitter or enjoy plain. Best served warm with a cup of lemon and lavender tea.

The Kitchen Witch is humming...
"Lovegood" —Alexandre Desplat

Mini Lemon Meringue Pies

Dudley helped himself to at least four slices of lemon meringue pie during Aunt Marge's visit in *Prisoner of Azkaban*. Infused with lime leaves and yuzu, these delicious lemon curd pies will have you swelling up with pride no matter the occasion.

PREP TIME 5 minutes COOK TIME 3 hour YIELD 10 mini lemon meringue pies

INGREDIENTS

SHORTCRUST PASTRY

- 2¾ cups plus 1 Tbsp (350 g) all-purpose flour
- ½ cup (100 g) granulated sugar
- Zest of 1 lemon
- Pinch of salt
- ¾ cup (170 g) chilled vegan butter, cubed
- 1 tsp (5 ml) vanilla extract
- 2 Tbsp (30 ml) oat milk, cold

LEMON CURD

- 1 vanilla pod
- Zest and juice of 6 lemons
- Zest and juice of 1 lime
- 1¼ cups (250 g) granulated sugar
- 2 lime leaves
- 1 tsp (2 g) turmeric powder
- ¼ tsp (0.5 g) yuzu powder
- 3 Tbsp plus 1 tsp (50 ml) orange mango oat milk
- 3 Tbsp (28 g) cornstarch
- Pinch of salt
- ½ cup (115 g) vegan butter, fridge cold

MERINGUE

- 1¼ cups (300 ml) aquafaba
- ⅓ cup (80 ml) water
- 1¼ cups (250 g) granulated sugar
- Zest of 1 lime
- ¼ tsp (0.5 g) yuzu powder
- 1½ tsp (3 g) agar agar powder
- 1 tsp (3 ml) vanilla extract
- Pinch of salt

GARNISH

- Edible flowers
- Mint leaves

MAGICAL METHOD

1. In a large mixing bowl, mix the dry pastry ingredients—flour, sugar, lemon zest and salt—with a fork until combined. Transfer to a food processor, then add the vegan butter and pulse until well incorporated.

2. Pour in the vanilla extract and the oat milk. Pulse again until a

dough forms (do not overmix).

3. Flatten the dough, shape it into a disc, wrap in cling wrap and refrigerate for 1 hour or overnight.

4. Meanwhile, start the lemon curd. Slice the vanilla pod in half and scrape out the seeds with the back of a knife.

5. In a medium saucepan on medium-high heat, add the lemon and lime juices and zests and stir in the sugar. Stir in the vanilla seeds and lime leaves. Simmer for 4 to 5 minutes, then whisk in the turmeric and yuzu.

6. In a small mixing bowl, combine the milk and cornstarch and whisk until smooth, then whisk into the saucepan until combined. Cook for 3 to 4 minutes, then turn off the heat. Sprinkle with salt, add the vegan butter and stir. Transfer to a jar and let cool completely.

7. Start the meringue. In a small saucepan on medium-high heat, cook the aquafaba for 8 to 10 minutes until it reduces by half.

8. Clean the stand mixer bowl and whisk attachment with lemon juice. If there is any greasiness or fat on the bowl or whisk, it will prevent the aquafaba from whipping up as it should. Pour in the aquafaba and whisk until the mixture becomes whiter and foamy. Aquafaba takes a long time to foam up, around 20 minutes. Keep the faith. When the aquafaba looks like a shiny cloud, turn off the mixer.

9. In a small saucepan on medium-high, combine the water, sugar, lime zest, yuzu powder and agar agar powder. Using a sugar thermometer, cook the mixture until it reaches 250 degrees F (121 degrees C). Turn off the heat. While the stand mixer is mixing the meringue on medium-low speed, slowly and carefully pour in the syrup (be careful—it might splatter). If you can hold the bowl upside-down without anything falling or sliding out, the meringue is ready.

10. Add the vanilla extract and a pinch of salt, and mix gently with a spatula.

11. Put the mini tart pans in the freezer for 10 to 15 minutes to minimize shrinking of the pastry.

12. Transfer the meringue to a prepared piping bag with a star piping tip. **TIP:** Folding the sides over and reaching into the bag to pour in the meringue mixture makes for less of a sticky mess. Twist the end of the bag closed and refrigerate until needed.

13. Remove the chilled dough from the fridge and either place it between two pieces of parchment paper or onto a floured work surface. Roll the dough to a thickness of about ½ inch (1.5 cm). Transfer the dough into the greased tart pans.

14. Preheat oven to 340 degrees F (170 degrees C).

15. Prick a few holes into the bottom of each tart with a fork. Trim any excess dough hanging off the pan, then tuck in the sides. Place the tarts back in the fridge for another 15 minutes.

16. Place a piece of parchment paper onto each tart and pour baking beans on top. Press down gently, then blind bake for 15 minutes. Brush some vegan butter onto the pastry, spreading evenly, and bake for 15 minutes. Let cool completely.

17. Fill each of the tarts with lemon curd, then pipe either one large dollop or several stars of meringue on top.

18. Using a crème brûlée torch, caramelize the meringues until they resemble s'mores and have a good color.

19. Garnish the tarts with edible flowers and mint leaves. Best enjoyed with a lovely cup of English lemon tea.

....

The Kitchen Witch is humming...
"Aunt Marge's Waltz"
—John Williams

....

From the Kitchen Witch

Feel free to revamp this recipe by swapping out the lemons for limes or passionfruit. To make your life easier, the lemon curd can be prepared a day beforehand.

Happee Birthdae Cake

Huddled with the Dursleys in the hut on the rock, Harry receives the birthday surprise of a lifetime in *Sorcerer's Stone*. Hagrid arrives with a generously frosted chocolate cake and news that'll change Harry's life forever. "Happee Birthdae" indeed.

PREP TIME 10 minutes **COOK TIME** 2 hours 30 minutes **YIELD** Enough for 10–12 witches and wizards

INGREDIENTS

VEGAN CHOCOLATE CAKE

- 2 cups (500 ml) oat milk
- 2 Tbsp (30 ml) lemon juice
- ¾ cup (150 g) softened vegan butter
- 2¼ cups (495 g) light brown sugar
- 1 Tbsp (10 g) orange marmalade
  Zest of 1 orange
- 1 Tbsp (15 ml) vanilla extract
- 2¾ cups plus 2 Tbsp (360 g) all-purpose flour
- 1 Tbsp (10 g) baking soda
- ½ tsp (1 g) sea salt
- ¾ cup plus 1 Tbsp (90 g) cacao powder
- ¼ cup (50 g) instant coffee
- 2 tsp (4 g) ground cinnamon

RASPBERRY FILLING

- 2 cups (250 g) fresh or frozen raspberries
- 1 tsp (5 ml) vanilla extract
- 2 Tbsp (20 g) chia seeds
- 1 tsp (2 g) ground ginger
- 1 tsp (2 g) ground cinnamon
- ¼ tsp (0.5 g) ground cardamom
- ¼ cup (85 g) maple syrup
  Zest and juice of 1 lemon

VEGAN BUTTERCREAM

- 2¾ cups plus 3 Tbsp (660 g) vegan butter, room temperature
- 1 Tbsp (15 ml) vanilla extract
  Zest of 2 limes
- ¾ cup plus 2 Tbsp (200 g) natural vegan cream cheese, room temperature
- 6 cups (750 g) icing sugar
- 1 Tbsp (15 ml) oat milk or lime juice
- 1 tsp (2 g) pink natural food coloring or beetroot powder

GREEN ICING

¾ **cup plus 1 Tbsp (100 g) powdered sugar**
1 **tsp (5 ml) vanilla extract**
2 **tsp (4 g) green matcha or spirulina**
Zest and juice of 1 lime

MAGICAL METHOD

1. Preheat oven to 355 degrees F (180 degrees C). Grease a baking pan with vegan butter, then line it with parchment paper. Set aside.
2. In a large jug, combine the oat milk and the lemon juice. Mix and set aside to let the milk curdle.
3. In a large mixing bowl or stand mixer bowl, add the vegan butter, sugar, orange marmalade, orange zest and vanilla extract. Set mixer on medium-high and whip until the mixture becomes pale and fluffy, about 5 to 6 minutes.
4. In a separate mixing bowl, combine the dry ingredients: flour, baking soda, salt, cacao powder, instant coffee and cinnamon. Whisk until fully combined with no lumps.
5. Set the mixer on a lower speed. Using a wooden spoon, add two spoonfuls of the dry ingredients to the first mixing bowl. Once this is combined, add a few splashes of oat milk. Repeat these steps until both elements are finished (ending with the dry ingredients).
6. Transfer the batter with a spatula to the lined baking pan and use a palette knife to level

the top. Tap the baking pan once against the counter to release any air bubbles.
7. Bake for 45 minutes until risen and fluffy. Let cool completely.
8. Get a medium-sized saucepan and add the raspberries, vanilla, chia seeds, ground spices, maple syrup and lemon zest and juice.
9. Heat to medium-high and stir everything until combined. Break up the raspberries with your wooden spoon to speed up the process.
10. Let the filling bubble away for 10 to 15 minutes until thickened. Stir occasionally. Let cool completely before adding to the cake.
11. In a large mixing bowl, add the vegan butter. Set mixer on medium-high speed. Beat until pale and fluffy, about 6 to 7 minutes. Add vanilla extract, lime zest and vegan cream cheese. Mix for 4 to 5 minutes.
12. Set mixer on low speed. Add half the icing sugar. Mix until fully incorporated, then add the rest. Next, add the oat milk and beetroot powder. Beat for 2 minutes. Set aside.
13. Slice the cake in half horizontally to create two layers. Place the bottom layer on a serving platter.
14. Top with 2 Tbsp of vegan buttercream, making sure to spread evenly, then layer on the raspberry filling. Next, place the

second cake half on top and gently press down.
15. Frost the cake with the remaining buttercream icing, starting from the top and working your way down the sides. Smooth out the icing evenly with the palette knife, but remember: no need to make it absolutely perfect—it's Hagrid's cake, after all.
16. In a medium-sized mixing bowl, add the powdered sugar. Stir in the vanilla extract, matcha or spirulina and lime zest and juice.
17. Whisk until smooth. Transfer the icing to a prepared piping bag with a small tip and write your "Happee Birthdae" message in the wonkiest lettering you can manage.
18. Serve immediately or carefully place in a white cake box and give to a dear friend.

....

The Kitchen Witch is humming…
"The Arrival of Baby Harry"
—John Williams

....

From the Kitchen Witch

Not a fan of raspberries? Strawberries, blueberries or blackberries will also do the trick, and stand up well to the chocolate cake.

Pumpkin Pasties

In *Sorcerer's Stone*, when the trolley witch asks, "Anything off the cart, dears?" and poor Ron looks disappointedly at his packed sandwiches, Harry indulges his friend and buys some of the witch's whole lot of snacks, including Pumpkin Pasties. Packed with a roasted spiced pumpkin filling, these traditional pastries make for the perfect on-the-go treat for the memorable journey to Hogwarts.

PREP TIME 10 minutes COOK TIME 40 minutes YIELD 12–14 Pumpkin Pasties

INGREDIENTS

SHORTCRUST PASTRY

- 2 cups (250 g) all-purpose flour
- 1 Tbsp (12 g) granulated sugar
- ¼ tsp (0.5 g) turmeric powder
- Pinch of salt
- ½ cup plus 1 Tbsp (125 g) vegan butter, cubed
- 2 Tbsp (30 ml) almond milk
- 1 Tbsp (15 ml) ice-cold water

PUMPKIN FILLING

- 3½ cups plus 1 Tbsp (500 g) pumpkin, cubed
- 1 Tbsp (15 ml) melted coconut oil
- 1½ tsp (3 g) Chinese seven spice
- 2 Tbsp (30 ml) vegan butter
- 1 Tbsp (21 g) maple syrup
- 1 tsp (5 ml) vanilla extract
- 1 tsp (2 g) cinnamon
- 1 Tbsp (10 g) coconut sugar, plus more for sprinkling
- 1 Tbsp (10 g) freshly grated ginger
- Zest of 1 orange
- ½ cup roasted pecans, optional

PASTRY COATING

- 1 Tbsp (15 ml) almond milk
- 1 tsp (3 ml) maple syrup

MAGICAL METHOD

1. In a large mixing bowl, mix the dry shortcrust ingredients with a fork. Mix in the vegan butter until you achieve the consistency of wet sand.

2. Pour in the milk and cold water. Mix until the dough comes together. Do not overmix!

3. Wrap the dough in cling wrap and refrigerate for 1 hour.

4. Preheat oven to 425 degrees F (220 degrees C). Line a baking sheet with parchment paper.

5. Place the cubed pumpkin on the baking sheet. Add the coconut oil and Chinese seven spice, mixing with your hands until incorporated.

6. Bake for 25 to 30 minutes until golden brown. Let cool.

7. Meanwhile, in a small saucepan, melt vegan butter on medium-low heat for 1 to 2 minutes. Pour in the maple syrup and vanilla extract. Mix until combined. Turn off the heat and mix in the cinnamon, coconut sugar and freshly grated ginger. Set aside.

8. Mash the roasted pumpkin with a fork and pour in the spiced vegan butter. Mix until combined, then stir in the orange zest and pecans (if using).

9. Preheat oven to 355 degrees F (180 degrees C).

10. Sprinkle flour over your kitchen surface, then roll out the dough to a thickness of about 0.5 cm. Use a cookie cutter to cut out as many circles as possible.

11. Add 1 Tbsp of pumpkin filling in the middle of each circle. Rub the edge of each circle with a little water, then fold each circle over to create half-moon-shaped pasties. Press the edge of the dough with a fork to seal. Combine the almond milk and maple syrup and brush the pasties with the mixture. Sprinkle with coconut sugar.

12. Bake for 25 minutes until golden brown. Best served slightly warm en route to adventure.

....

The Kitchen Witch is humming…
"Platform Nine-and-Three-Quarters and the Journey to Hogwarts"
    —*John Williams*

....

From the Kitchen Witch

Liven up these pasties by creating a fun pattern on top or cut three slits to let through more steam so the pasties won't crack on top.

Exploding Bonbons

Named for the sweets sold at Honeydukes during Harry's first visit in
Prisoner of Azkaban, these white chocolate bonbons are bursting with sweet pineapple,
zesty orange, a hint of mint and a surprising kiss of rose.
A pinch of popping sugar lends these confections their signature sizzle.

PREP TIME 5 minutes   COOK TIME 35 minutes   YIELD 10 huge bonbons

INGREDIENTS

FILLING

- ½ cup (70 g) freeze-dried raspberries
- ½ tsp (2.5 ml) rose water
-   Zest of 1 orange
- 1 cup (120 g) vegan coconut biscuits
- ½ cup (115 g) white almond butter
- ½ cup (82 g) dried pineapple
- ½ tsp (1 g) dried mint
-   Pinch of sea salt
- ¼ cup (50 g) popping sugar

BONBONS

- 2 cups plus 4 Tbsp (400 g) vegan white chocolate

MAGICAL METHOD

1. Add all filling ingredients except popping sugar to a food processor. Blend until combined. Transfer to a large mixing bowl, add the popping sugar, mix until combined and set aside.

2. Using the double boiler method, melt and temper the white chocolate (for instructions, see pg. 187).

3. Fill each well of a bonbon mold with 2 Tbsp of melted chocolate. Place in the fridge and let set for at least 10 minutes.

4. Add 1½ Tbsp of filling into each, then cover with more chocolate. Tap the mold on the counter to release any air bubbles, then transfer to the fridge for at least 2 hours.

5. Carefully flip out the bonbons and wrap them individually or eat right away.

....

The Kitchen Witch is humming…
"Fireworks" —Nicholas Hooper

....

From the Kitchen Witch

This recipe works well with vegan dark chocolate, too! Unable to find vegan popping sugar?
Mix 50 g rock sugar with ½ tsp baking soda, ¼ tsp citric acid and zest of half a lemon.

Chocolate Frogs

Harry's trove of mouthwatering confections on the Hogwarts Express in *Sorcerer's Stone* includes Chocolate Frogs. Made with 70 percent chocolate and finished with a touch of sea salt, these artisanal amphibians won't hop away before you gobble them up.

PREP TIME 5 minutes   **COOK TIME** 30 minutes   **YIELD** 10–12 Chocolate Frogs

INGREDIENTS

- 1½ cups plus 3 Tbsp (300 g) rice milk chocolate
- 1 Tbsp (10 g) cacao nibs
- 2 Tbsp (30 g) raisins
- Pinch of sea salt

MAGICAL METHOD

1. Finely chop the milk chocolate. Reserve ½ cup (75 g) for later.

2. To melt the chocolate using the double boiler method: Fill one-third of a small saucepan with water and bring to medium-low heat. Place a well-fitting heatproof bowl on top, then add the chocolate. Cook until it reaches 115 degrees F (45 degrees C). Remove bowl from heat.

3. Stir in reserved chocolate. The mixture should read 87.8 degrees F (31 degrees C) on a thermometer.

4. Transfer the melted chocolate onto a marble cutting board. Using a palette knife, guide the chocolate over the board. When the chocolate becomes slightly thicker and shiny, remove it from the marble and pour it into the frog molds, leaving room at the top for the other ingredients.

5. Sprinkle each well with cacao nibs and raisins, pushing down slightly. Add a sprinkle of sea salt.

6. Let the chocolate sit at room temperature for 10 to 15 minutes then refrigerate for 1 hour.

7. Tap out the chocolate frogs onto a serving platter or place in individual Chocolate Frog boxes and pack for your journey to Hogwarts.

The Kitchen Witch is humming…
"A Journey to Hogwarts"
—*Nicholas Hooper*

From the Kitchen Witch

The technique of melting the chocolate on a cold marble board is called tempering. This makes the chocolate beautiful and shiny. Best of all, it will have a real snap when you bite into it and won't melt in your hands. The Kitchen Witch prefers Croatian chocolate if you can get your hands on some.

Iced White Chocolate Truffles

When Harry attends the Yule Ball in *Goblet of Fire*, the Great Hall is decked out in a spectacular wash of silver and shimmering ice. Dusted in edible metallic luster, these charming confections make for a tempting centerpiece no matter the occasion.

PREP TIME 5 minutes   COOK TIME 25 minutes to overnight   YIELD 30 truffles

INGREDIENTS

- 1 cup plus 2 Tbsp (200 g) vegan white chocolate, finely chopped
- 1¼ cups (300 ml) coconut cream
- 3 lime leaves
- ¼ tsp (0.5 g) fennel seeds
- Zest of 1 lime
- 2 Tbsp (30 ml) vegan Baileys
- 1 tsp (5 ml) vanilla extract
- ½ cup (15 g) freeze-dried bananas
- ¼ tsp (0.5 g) ground cardamom
- ½ cup (57 g) hazelnuts, finely chopped
- Pinch of sea salt
- ½ cup (140 g) white cashew butter

COATING

- 1½ cups (120 g) shredded coconut
- 1½ cups (120 g) coconut flakes
- Edible silver luster dust

MAGICAL METHOD

1. To melt the chocolate using the double boiler method, fill one-third of a small saucepan with water and set on medium-low heat. Place a well-fitting heatproof bowl on top, then add the chocolate. Cook for 7 to 8 minutes, stirring occasionally.

2. Meanwhile, in a medium saucepan on medium-high heat, add the coconut cream, lime leaves and fennel seeds. Simmer for about 10 to 15 minutes. Remove from heat, pour the mixture through a sieve to remove the leaves and seeds and let cool to room temperature.

3. Whisk the melted white chocolate into the mixture until combined. Stir in the lime zest, Baileys and vanilla extract. Tear up the freeze-dried bananas (or blend to a fine crumb in a food processor) and add to the truffle mixture along with cardamom, hazelnuts and sea salt.

4. Stir in the cashew butter and mix until combined. Refrigerate for at least 2 hours or overnight.

5. Roll the hardened truffle mixture into small balls, about as large as a Golden Snitch.

6. In a small mixing bowl, combine the shredded coconut, coconut flakes and silver luster dust. Coat the truffles in the topping and serve.

....

The Kitchen Witch is humming…
"Neville's Waltz" —Patrick Doyle
....

From the Kitchen Witch

Unable to find freeze-dried banana? Banana chips, dried apricots or dried mango do the trick.

Pumpkin Patch Brownies

The conversation might always be great at the half-giant's hut, but as we know from *Sorcerer's Stone*, the snacks are little more than rock cakes. If he'd looked to the pumpkin patch just outside, Hagrid might've thought to whip up these golden, toothsome treats.

PREP TIME 5 minutes **COOK TIME** 45 minutes **YIELD** Enough for 6–8 magical friends

INGREDIENTS

PUMPKIN SWIRL

- ¼ cup (40 g) cubed pumpkin
- 1 tsp (5 ml) melted coconut oil
- ½ tsp (1 g) gingerbread spices
- ¼ cup (60 g) vegan cream cheese
- 1 Tbsp (10 g) coconut sugar

BROWNIE BATTER

- 1 tsp (2 g) espresso powder
- 1 tsp (2 g) ground cinnamon
  Pinch of sea salt
- 1 cup (220 g) light brown sugar
- 1 cup (125 g) all-purpose flour
- 1 tsp (2 g) baking powder
- ¾ cup (82 g) cacao powder
- ½ cup (125 ml) vegan butter, melted
- 1 tsp (5 ml) vanilla extract
- ⅓ cup (80 ml) oat milk
- 6 Tbsp (93 g) applesauce
- ¼ cup (85 g) maple syrup
- 1 cup (240 g) vegan dark chocolate chips, divided

MAGICAL METHOD

1. Preheat oven to 430 degrees F (220 degrees C). Line a baking sheet with parchment paper.

2. Place the cubed pumpkin on the baking sheet. Add the melted coconut oil and gingerbread spices, mixing with your hands until incorporated. Roast for 15 to 20 minutes or until soft and fragrant. Let cool completely.

3. Add the roasted pumpkin, vegan cream cheese and coconut sugar to a blender or food processor. Blend until smooth, then refrigerate until needed.

4. Set oven to 345 degrees F (175 degrees C).

5. In a large mixing bowl, add the dry ingredients, making sure to sift the flour, cacao and baking powder. Mix until combined.

6. In a small saucepan on medium heat, melt the vegan butter. Let cool slightly before using.

7. Make a well in the center of the dry ingredients, then pour in the vanilla extract, oat milk and melted butter. Spoon in the apple sauce and maple syrup. Using a spatula, mix until combined (but do not overmix).

8. Add half the chocolate chips to the batter and stir until combined. Transfer the batter to a greased baking pan and spread evenly.

9. Place 6 to 7 dollops of the chilled pumpkin swirl onto the brownie batter. Using a chopstick, swirl the ingredients to create a marbled effect. Sprinkle the remaining chocolate chips on top.

10. Bake for 25 minutes until fudgy and gorgeous.

11. Let the brownies completely cool before cutting into delectable squares.

....

The Kitchen Witch is humming…
"Hagrid the Professor" —John Williams

....

From the Kitchen Witch

Add clementine zest to the pumpkin swirl for an extra festive touch.

Handmade Dragon Eggs

In *Sorcerer's Stone*, Hagrid hatches a dragon's egg he won from a stranger at the Hog's Head Inn. Celebrate Norbert(a)'s birth by making these sweet and spicy coconut egg-shaped delights to share by the light of a crackling fire.

PREP TIME 5 minutes   **COOK TIME** 35 minutes   **YIELD** 30 dragon eggs

INGREDIENTS

DRAGON EGGS

- 2 cups (192 g) shredded coconut
- 2 tsp (4 g) stem ginger, chopped
- ½ cup (90 g) dried mango, chopped
- Zest of 1 lime
- 1 tsp (5 ml) vanilla extract
- Pinch of salt
- ½ cup plus 1 Tbsp (135 ml) condensed coconut milk
- ¼ tsp (0.5 g) ground cardamom

DIP

- 1½ cups (255 g) dark chocolate (87%), finely chopped
- ½ tsp (1 g) chile flakes
- Pinch of sea salt

COATING

- 2½ cups (82 g) pandan rice flakes
- Edible gold and silver luster dust, optional
- Blue spirulina, optional
- Matcha powder, optional
- Freeze-dried raspberry powder, optional

MAGICAL METHOD

1. In a mixing bowl, combine the coconut, stem ginger, dried mango, lime zest, vanilla extract, salt, condensed coconut milk and cardamom, stirring well. Refrigerate until needed.

2. To melt the chocolate using the double boiler method, fill one-third of a small saucepan with water and set to medium-low heat. Place a well-fitting heatproof bowl on top, then add the chocolate, reserving 2 Tbsp. Cook until it reaches 115 degrees F (45 degrees C). Remove the bowl from the heat and place on a cutting board or kitchen surface.

3. Stir the reserved 2 Tbsp into the melted chocolate. At this point, the mixture should read 87.8 degrees F (31 degrees C) on a thermometer.

4. Transfer the melted chocolate onto a marble cutting board and guide the chocolate over the board with a palette knife. When the chocolate becomes slightly thicker and shiny, remove it from the marble cutting board. Mix in the chile flakes and salt.

5. Using the back of a spoon, press 1½ tsp (8 g) of the coconut mixture into each well of the egg mold. Place the mold in the freezer to set for 5 minutes.

6. Carefully remove the egg halves from the molds. Join the halves together and shape as desired.

7. Dip each egg one by one into the chocolate, then into the rice flakes. Refrigerate eggs for 10 minutes before serving.

8. Serve with a wonderful cup of hot and spicy chocolate.

....

The Kitchen Witch is humming…
"The Norwegian Ridgeback and a Change of Season" —John Williams

....

From the Kitchen Witch

Sliced almonds or corn flakes make for an equally crunchy alternative for coating the dragon eggs.

Salted Dark Chocolate and Caramel Honeycomb

When Harry wasn't allowed to go to Hogsmeade in *Prisoner of Azkaban*,
he donned the Invisibility Cloak and traversed the secret passage
that led straight to Honeydukes, where a world of incredible sweets awaited him.
Enrobed in dark chocolate, these crunchy treats are exactly the kind of
old-fashioned treat you might find in the wizarding village's beloved candy shop.

PREP TIME 5 minutes **COOK TIME** 15 minutes **YIELD** Enough for 6–8 witches and wizards with a sweet tooth

INGREDIENTS

HONEYCOMB

- ¾ cup (250 g) golden syrup
- 1¼ cups (250 g) granulated sugar
- 1 tsp (5 ml) vanilla extract
- 1 tsp (2 g) ground cinnamon
- ¼ tsp (0.5 g) ground nutmeg
- ½ tsp (1 g) ground ginger
- 3¼ tsp (15 g) baking soda

DARK CHOCOLATE DIP

- ¾ cup (127.5 g) dark chocolate (87%), finely chopped
- 1 tsp (5 ml) coconut oil
- Pinch of sea salt

MAGICAL METHOD

1. Brush the baking pan with vegetable oil, then line with foil, tucking in the sides.

2. In a heavy-bottomed pan on medium-high heat, add all the honeycomb ingredients except the baking soda. Stir until combined and let the mixture come to a boil. Add a candy thermometer and let the mixture cook until it reaches 300.2 degrees F (150 degrees C), then remove from heat and quickly whisk in the baking soda.
Note: The mixture will bubble a lot, so be careful!

3. Wearing oven mitts, transfer the mixture to the lined baking pan with foil and let the honeycomb cool completely for at least 1 hour. Break the honeycomb into pieces.

4. Using the double boiler method on medium-low heat, melt the chocolate, then add the coconut oil and sea salt. Mix until combined.

5. Dip one side of each honeycomb shard into the chocolate, then place on a baking sheet lined with parchment paper to set at room temperature for 10 to 15 minutes.

6. Arrange on a serving platter. Best paired with a wonderful cup of ginger tea.

....

The Kitchen Witch is humming…
"Knockturn Alley" —John Williams
....

From the Kitchen Witch

A candy thermometer is mandatory for this recipe. Candy-making is a science, and the temperature must be exact.

MEMORY VIAL

My first time preparing honeycomb—before I perfected this recipe—was a mess. I added way too much baking soda, and the boiling caramel flooded over and around the pan, making for a very dangerous round of "the floor is lava."

Appendix

Conversion Guide

If you're a wizard who favors the metric system, this chart will help transmute cups and ounces to liters and grams.

Volume

¼ tsp	1 mL
½ tsp	2 mL
1 tsp	5 mL
1 Tbsp	15 mL
¼ cup	50mL
⅓ cup	75 mL
½ cup	125 mL
⅔ cup	150 mL
¾ cup	175 mL
1 cup	250 mL
1 quart	1 liter
1½ quarts	1.5 liters
2 quarts	2 liters
2½ quarts	2.5 liters
3 quarts	3 liters
4 quarts	4 liters

Temperature

32° F	0° C
212° F	100° C
250° F	120° C
275° F	140° C
300° F	150° C
325° F	160° C
350° F	180° C
375° F	190° C
400° F	200° C
425° F	220° C
450° F	230° C
475° F	240° C
500° F	260° C

Length

⅛ in	3 mm
¼ in	6 mm
½ in	13 mm
¾ in	19 mm
1 in	2.5 cm
2 in	5 cm

Weight

1 oz	30 g
2 oz	55 g
3 oz	85 g
4 oz / ¼ lb	115 g
8 oz / ½ lb	225 g
16 oz / 1 lb	455 g
32 oz / 2 lb	910 g

Mince Pies,
pg. 162

Acknowledgments

IMANA GRASHUIS

A sincere thank you to my mother, Signalda, for your unconditional support, your passionate creativity, assisting me with every creation I captured and reliving with me the timeless dishes created during the production of this cookbook.

I'd also like to extend my heartfelt gratitude to my father, Leo, for agreeing to take every crazy idea I had for styling props and bring them to fruition. Your belief in me gave me the strength to put every ounce of energy I had into every creation.

A special thank you to Chanel for finding the most magical styling props that I could ever dream of. Your support means the world to me and your thrift queen skills transported every creation to the wizarding world.

Thank you to Chantal from Huize Druivelaar for letting me shoot at your breathtaking greenhouse to transport readers to Herbology class. Your kindness is much appreciated.

A deeply heartfelt thank you to Tylor for making this absolute vegan *Harry Potter* dream come true. Your friendship means so much to me.

And last but not least, a special thank you to my best mate, Koen, for your unwavering support.

TYLOR STARR

I would like to thank my ever-supporting partner, Danielle, for all of her patience, love and encouragement.

I would also like to thank my family, James, Samantha, Jessica, Levi and Lily, for always supporting my obsession with *Harry Potter*. A heartfelt thank you to Evanna Lynch, Kathryn Henzler, Jordan Page, Valerie Short, Ken Montville, Kat Miller, Ali Matthews, Katie Johnson, Claire Jacobmeyer, Danielle Reicherter, Grant Hurlbert and everyone else who has ever worked at or supported The Protego Foundation.

And finally, I would like to thank Imana Grashuis for agreeing to co-author this book and for the delicious magic she shares with the world.

Arthur's
Eggnog,
pg. 158

Index

About the Authors

IMANA GRASHUIS is the founder and soul behind *Magical Food Department*. A practicing Kitchen Witch from the Netherlands obsessed with the wizarding world, Imana is a full-time food photographer, stylist and recipe developer.

Emotions and scents have stuck in her memory from childhood and made her the Kitchen Witch she is today. The love for her heritage and her passion for witchcraft came together as one and forged a path where she creates dishes she wishes existed. This process has made for an explosion of work and creativity, a dream that nurtures her purpose to inspire others to try vegan food and heal the world through each recipe in an immersive way.

To follow Imana's work, visit *magicalfooddepartment.com*.

TYLOR STARR is the world's foremost expert on Animal Rights in the Wizarding World fan activism, creator and co-founder of the wizarding-inspired animal rights charity The Protego Foundation, co-host of *The ChickPeeps* vegan podcast and producer of the *Radicals and Revolutionaries* podcast.

Tylor's full-time work in animal rights began in 2012 when he joined PETA working in youth outreach as a senior strategist to mobilize young people for animal liberation. He currently lives in his hometown of Greeley, Colorado, with his partner, Danielle, and their beloved rescue pup, Roxy.

To follow Tylor's work, visit *tylorstarr.com*.

EVANNA LYNCH is an actress, writer and podcaster. Her professional career began at the age of 14 when she began playing the role of Luna Lovegood in the *Harry Potter* film series. A lifelong animal lover, Evanna went vegan in 2013 and in 2017 launched a vegan podcast, *The ChickPeeps*, to explore veganism in a friendly, fun, accessible way. She began her literary journey in October 2021 by publishing her memoir, *The Opposite of Butterfly Hunting: The Tragedy and the Glory of Growing Up.* She lives in London with her cat friend, Puff, where she divides her time between performing, writing and animal rights activism.

Project management and proofreading witchcraft provided by Jordan Page.

About The Protego Foundation

Since its inception, The Protego Foundation has been at the forefront of Animal Rights in the Wizarding World fan activism. When Tylor Starr and Kathryn Henzler first founded the organization in 2015, they imagined a way in which they could harness the empathy and energy of *Harry Potter* fans to make the non-magical world a kinder, more compassionate place for all creatures, regardless of species, size or magical ability. Using wizarding world-inspired analogies, The Protego Foundation has created many campaigns and programs over the years that have brought about positive change for animals in need. With a team of more than 25 volunteers and 5,400 members and supporters worldwide, The Protego Foundation's reach is greater than ever before.

The group also runs community-building programs like the *ProtegoCast* podcast and our monthly book club to encourage fans to think critically about how animals are treated in the media we consume as well as in real life. The Protego Foundation is both proud and honored to be a beneficiary of the release of this *Harry Potter*-inspired vegan cookbook. We hope that with this book in the hands of magical fans around the world, it can motivate more people to embrace a lifestyle that is friendlier to animals and to their rights as living beings—because all creatures are magical.

Thank you for purchasing this book and in turn supporting the work we do to make the world a more magical place for all animals.

For more information, visit *protegofoundation.org*.

Media Lab Books
For inquiries, call 646-449-8614

Copyright © 2022 by Tylor Starr

Published by Topix Media Lab
14 Wall Street, Suite 3C
New York, NY 10005

Printed in China

ISBN-13: 978-1-956403-06-0
ISBN-10: 1-956403-06-X

Additional art: Shutterstock

Indexing by R studio T, NYC

1C-G22-1